The Early History of
Sunland, California:
Volumes 1-8

*A compilation of the eight previously
published volumes in the series
The Early History of Sunland, California.*

ML Tiernan

The Early History of Sunland, California

www.maryleetiernan.com
First printing April, 2015
10 9 8 7 6 5 4 3 2 1

ISBN 978-1511680288 (Paperback)

Photograph on cover courtesy of Bolton Hall Museum, Tujunga, California.

Contents

Author's Notes

The researcher, like a detective, examines the evidence to try to determine the real story. Unfortunately for researchers, we cannot re-examine witnesses or revisit scenes because in most cases, they have long since disappeared. So we sort through the conflicting data to find the most reliable and logical explanations. I have done my best to follow the clues and weave as authentic a story as possible.

My thanks to the staff at Bolton Hall Museum, Tujunga, California, for their assistance with this project.

Hotels
for the Hopeful

**"No frosts! No fogs!
Splendid soil! Perfect climate!
Abundance of pure mountain water!
The most beautiful mountain resort in California!"**

*The Early History of Sunland, California
Volume 1*

ML Tiernan

Land promoters of the 1880s promised a perfect life of health, wealth, and pleasure in Monte Vista. Although their promises fell short of reality, the village did grow and prosper in the hands of farmers and was renamed Sunland.

Hotels for the Hopeful

*Land promoters promise a perfect life
of health, wealth, and pleasure
in Monte Vista.*

**The Early History of Sunland, California
Volume 1**

ML Tiernan

Hotels for the Hopeful

www.maryleetiernan.com
Second printing April 1, 2015
10 9 8 7 6 5 4 3 2

ISBN 978-0983067207 (Paperback)

Photograph on cover courtesy of Bolton Hall Museum,
Tujunga, California.
Quote on cover from advertisements for Monte Vista.

Contents

The Land Boom of the 1880s

When the Southern Pacific Railroad finished the line connecting Los Angeles to San Francisco in 1876, it completed the last leg of the transcontinental railroad. The timing was perfect. After the Civil War, people began migrating westward. The real estate boom in the Midwest had just about run its course when the Southern Pacific provided access to even more new territory by opening Southern California for settlement. Spying the opportunity for new fortunes, speculators rushed to California. "They came here not to build up the country, but to make money, honestly, if they could not make it any other way."[1]

These veteran promoters would create the impression of a town-in-progress by building a hotel and laying sidewalks or curbs. Often they began construction on bogus railroad stations because a railroad line through town promised future prosperity. Smooth-talking, confident, and unrestrained by honesty, they sold lots in towns built of air. Between 1884 and 1886, speculators platted 100 towns in Los Angeles County; 62 of them no longer exist.

Because the railroad companies needed to recoup the fortune spent in building lines across the desert, and because they wanted to ensure future business and profit, they eagerly encouraged the westward migration. They hired agents who hawked the glories of California across the United States and Europe. Special emigrant cars carried hopefuls to the 'promised land.' Because trains dropped the dining cars once they passed the Mississippi River, passengers brought bread and food in tins with them. A stove in the rear of the car allowed travelers to heat water or make coffee. For sleeping, the seats folded out into beds. To alleviate the harshness of travel, the train stopped during the day to allow passengers to exercise. Some trains carried entertainers or a clergyman for Sunday services. The railroad also furnished excursion trains for larger groups seeking to settle a colony.

But the opening of a second line, the Santa Fe, in 1886, broke the Southern Pacific's monopoly and sparked an explosion unparalleled elsewhere. Competition for passengers ignited a price war between the two companies. The usual rate of $125 for fare from Missouri to California began to drop. As one company decreased its price, the other undercut it. Prices fell drastically. On March 6, 1887, the Santa Fe actually reduced the fare to $1 per passenger.

Low rates inspired even more settlers, tourists, and sightseers to embark toward the Pacific shores and

California's glorious climate. After completion of the Southern Pacific, the population increased 100 times. After the Santa Fe line opened, the population multiplied 500 times. California exploded from 5,000 to 100,000 in only 20 years.

The avalanche of visitors accorded speculators golden opportunities for fleecing the public. Copywriters used alluring language, made wild promises, and even lied. In this war to attract prospective buyers, claims were as outlandish as the imagination allowed. One promoter went as far as sticking oranges on Joshua trees in the desert and

Sunland 1909 looking toward the entrance to Big Tujunga Canyon.
Photo courtesy of Bolton Hall Museum.

claimed they grew there naturally.

The ads for Monte Vista followed this same pattern. In one ad, the promoters promised, "Four miles only from the S.P.R.R. (Southern Pacific Railroad) and four railroads looking towards it with the certainty of one being built within a year, and no possibility of passing around it."[2] Of course, the railroad never materialized. One unusual difference in the promoters' approach was the construction of a working water system before plots were offered for sale. But ads exaggerated the abundance of water, the richness of the soil, and most of all, the climate, one of the prime attractions to California. Although the clean, clear air in Monte Vista really was good, who would believe that "The very instant the invalid reaches Monte Vista, improvement begins and continues until perfect health and strength are recovered. Who will not gain health here is beyond hope."[3]

But for all their efforts, they failed. When the land boom died at the end of the 1880s and the dust settled, Monte Vista was considered one of the towns that didn't make it. The farmers and entrepreneurs persevered, however, and eventually the village called Sunland thrived.

Simple Beginnings

When travelers descended from the train at Roscoe depot, they could walk the four and a half miles up Roscoe Blvd. to Monte Vista or take the 'stage.' Most, of course, chose the stage. Unlike the more elaborate version pictured in Western films, a simple horse and buggy escorted passengers over the rough roads. Even when a pickup truck, with wood benches running along the sides of the bed, later replaced the horse and buggy, one still referred

John Johnson (center) greeted visitors at his Monte Vista Inn after their dusty ride to the village. Photo Courtesy of Bolton Hall Museum.

to it as the 'stagecoach.'

As the stagecoach ascended the last knoll, Watson Hill, and cruised to the level land around the park, it stopped at John J. Johnson's Monte Vista Inn. In the early 1880s, Johnson converted a small hunting lodge into a public inn to greet visitors after the bumpy, difficult ride to the village.

In warm weather, John stood behind a counter under the shade of a large pine serving bottled drinks and snacks. Of course, ice wasn't available, but the drinks still refreshed thirsty throats after that dusty ride on dirt roads. Wooden benches around the base of the tree provided seating for his customers. The outside 'bar' stretched between the inn and his house.

John J. Johnson
Photo from Bolton Hall Museum

The inn's founder was the son of Farmer A. Johnson, one of the original homesteaders in the Monte Vista Valley. Like his father and brothers, John[4] homesteaded land in Big Tujunga Canyon, where he hived bees. But unlike his father and brothers who lived in the more remote canyon, John preferred living and

16

working in the center of town. Official records from 1911 show John paid a total of $4.11 in taxes on his two parcels of choice land across from Sunland Park.

Living in town allowed John to take advantage of improvements as the village grew. The telephone arrived in 1908, when 22 subscribers invested $2,200 to found the Sunland Rural Telephone Company. In the beginning, service was limited to one and a half hours each morning and evening. A single line ran up the valley from Glendale to the switchboard, housed in the home of the operator. With only one line, the whole village could tune in at the same time. Not much chance of privacy in those early days! But as the company grew, John and the other

The inn became a popular dance pavilion named Twin Pines in the 1920s.
Photo from The Record-Ledger, June 18, 1964.

shareholders would reap sizable financial rewards.

The inn served other purposes over the years as a post office, a confectionary store, an open-air theater, and a dance pavilion. When the outdoor pavilion opened in September 1923, the name of the inn changed to Twin Pines, a fitting tribute to the large trees growing on either side of the entrance. As the price of admission opening night, attendees donated a quart of fruit or jam to the home for underprivileged children then operating at the Monte Vista Hotel. Dancing continued at the inn, or Twin Pines, until 1931.

When John died two years later in 1933, his property

Bulldozers crushed the old inn just short of its 100th birthday.
The name was still visible on the worn wood.
Photo from of The Record-Ledger, June 18, 1964.

passed on to his heirs. Eventually, they sold the property and the inn was condemned.

Bulldozers crushed the dilapidated Monte Vista Inn close to its 100th birthday in 1964. By then, boards covered the windows and doors, and very few traces of paint remained on the worn wood walls. Only the large letters spelling out the name of the inn were still visible.

Sunland Park in the 1880-1890s. Photo courtesy of Bolton Hall Museum.

The Park Hotel welcomed early visitors to Sunland.
Photo from The Record-Ledger, August 8, 1968.

Homestyle Hospitality

Anna Jump liked to sit in her rocking chair on the porch, a popular activity in times past, and watch life in town pass by. Her husband Sid preferred a more active routine, watering and pruning the gardens which surrounded the house. Inside, President Harding greeted visitors from the wall, pressed wood chairs awaited guests around the dining table, and a hand-wound Victrola played in the parlor. Basins and pitchers on the bureaus in the bedrooms offered the weary a chance to wash up before climbing into high iron beds to sleep. Such was the life in the Jump house in the 1960s!

The eight-room home, with four bedrooms upstairs and one bedroom and one bath downstairs, functioned as a hotel for almost 50 years. Sources conflict on the origin of the Park Hotel. Some sources credit Frank H. Barclay with building it as a home for his wife and three daughters, who lived there before the completion of his Monte Vista Hotel just down the street. Other sources credit Sherman Page and F.C. Howes, the original land speculators in the Monte Vista Valley, with its construction.

Page and Howes bought about 2,200 acres of the original Rancho Tujunga in 1883. That same year, they filed a claim for water rights to Big Tujunga Canyon and built a water system to divert water to their property. They platted 40 acres of the land for a town; the remaining acreage would be sold as farmland. In the center of the future town, a grove of majestic live oaks stretched their branches. They preserved an oval-shaped piece of the grove, bisecting Sherman and Central Avenues, for a park. On a site facing the oak grove park, they commissioned the building of a hotel where potential buyers could stay while inspecting the land. An ad in the *Rural Californian* dated

Rear view of the Park Hotel. Photo courtesy of Bolton Hall Museum.

November 1885 refers to that hotel when it promises that "All expenses incurred by purchase of land after leaving Los Angeles, including hack fare and hotel bills, will be deducted from the purchase price." Page and Howes named their village Monte Vista.

The only structure in early Monte Vista that could be Page and Howes' hotel is the Park Hotel. In addition, sources do agree that the building dates back to 1884 or 1885. It is more probable, therefore, that credit for its construction goes to Page and Howes. Barclay didn't buy the land from them until 1886[5] when construction on the Monte Vista Hotel began.

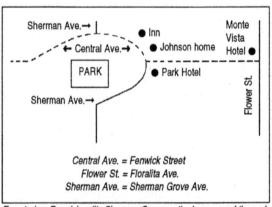

Even today, Fenwick splits Sherman Grove on the loop around the park.

The Park Hotel, on the corner of Central and Sherman Avenues, welcomed the earliest overnight visitors to Monte Vista. It faced the park from which it derived its name: originally referred to as Live Oak Park, the name changed to Monte Vista Park, then to Sunland Park. On the hotel's north side, just across the dirt road, stood the Monte Vista Inn.

After the Barclays moved out, Ben Willis and his wife, nicknamed Aunt Randy, managed the hotel. Publicity and news accounts often overlooked the smaller hotel, claiming the Monte Vista Hotel to be the first hotel, but not always. An advertisement for land sales in *The Los Angeles Times* from 1887 stresses accommodations in the larger and more luxurious Monte Vista Hotel, but mentions the "...Park Hotel, a smaller house, but equally neat and clean, but conducted on a lower scale of prices, faces the grand oak grove."[6] Rooms at the Park rented for $2.50 a night; those at the Monte Vista Hotel for $3 to $4 a night.

By 1906, Los Angeles had definitely established itself as a major Western city with all the conveniences a thriving metropolis can offer. Nevertheless, Anna Brandstetter and her husband sold their city home, packed up three-year-old Herbert, and headed for the largely unsettled Monte Vista Valley. Although considered a 'ghost town' by some historians because of its failure to establish itself during the boom of the 1880s, those who had moved to Monte Vista planted their feet as well as grapes and olives, peaches and apricots, oranges and lemons.

After buying the Park Hotel and a 13-acre farm, the Brandstetters adjusted to rustic life in the country. Only Rowley's General Store, and the butcher who came from San Fernando once a week to deliver fresh meat, offered the luxury of outside amenities. Just getting to the Roscoe train station often meant a four-and-a-half-mile walk.

While her husband tended the peach grove and vineyard, Anna cared for their home, their lodgers, and their son Herbert, one of only five children in the original Sunland school. Anna cooked and baked on a wood-burning stove, sewed her own clothes by the light of a kerosene lamp, and drew needed water from a well with a bucket. Their few hours of free time limited recreation to picnics in the park across the street. However grueling the life of those pioneer farmers, Anna later reminisced, "Perhaps I was foolish to leave my home in Los Angeles, but it was just what we wanted, and we were happy. I wish I had it back now."[7]

Several years later, the trees in their orchard stopped bearing fruit because of droughts and the increasing demand on the water supply from newcomers to the valley. The Brandstetters sold their farm acreage, but kept their home and continued welcoming guests. After Mr. Brandsetter died in 1924, Anna married Sidney (Sid) Jump. The doors to the Park Hotel stayed open into the 1930s when the Jumps retired. Townsfolk renamed the old

Park Hotel the Jump House because of Sid's familiar figure in the garden and Anna's on the porch, finally resting after her years of toil. Both died in 1965.

The 1971 earthquake shook the building until floors buckled, walls sloped at odd angles, and the porch jutted out over the front steps. The irreparable damage spelled death for the then-oldest structure in Sunland. A small apartment house replaced it.

Irreparable damage from the 1971 earthquake doomed the old house.
Photo from The Record-Ledger, February 14, 1971.

The Grand and Elegant

At the height of the land boom in 1887, $100 million worth of land sold in Los Angeles County alone. But by 1886, only a couple of dozen people had actually settled in Monte Vista, with about 250 acres of land under irrigation. Page and Howes were probably glad to unload their unsold land to Frank H. Barclay for a large profit. Unfortunately for Barclay, he bought toward the end of the boom.

Exaggerated advertising flourished during the 1880s as speculators competed with each other trying to attract buyers. Barclay's ads to entice visitors to Monte Vista followed that pattern. "…just right for the growing of all the finest California fruits … The air is absolutely pure and dry … delicate persons may hope for life, health and strength in the glorious climate of Monte Vista … (water) is absolutely pure and clear as crystal and practically unlimited."[8]

Barclay's imagination soared in his description of Monte Vista Park with "terraces planted in ornamental flowers and plants, while hammocks and swings, benches

**The elegant Monte Vista Hotel, pictured here just after its
construction, offered first class amenities to its guests.
Photo courtesy of Bolton Hall Museum.**

and chairs make attractions that elsewhere cannot be had,
while beautiful fountains make a delicious music for those
who are ill or those who are well."[9] In reality, the park was
then simply a grove of oak trees where Barclay and others
enjoyed excellent rabbit hunting.

The small Park Hotel seemed inadequate for the
crowds Barclay hoped to attract to Monte Vista. A larger,
more elegant hotel could not only house potential buyers,
but attract vacationers. So at the extravagant cost of
$30,000[10] Barclay started construction of the Monte Vista

Hotel on the corner of Central Avenue (Fenwick Street) and Flower (Floralita) Avenue in 1886. When it opened in 1887, an advertisement described the Monte Vista Hotel as "...the most charming resort ... Absolutely first-class in every detail ... nothing is left undone to make it absolutely a model hotel."[11] This, at least, was true.

The luxurious Victorian offered comfort in elegantly furnished rooms; each room featured a fireplace for warmth, and ventilation for hot days. Amenities included gas lighting, a fire-alarm system, a large dining room with a pine dance floor, service with fine china and silver, and a unique two-story privy. The observatory on the tower offered a panoramic view of the valley, or guests could relax on the twelve-foot-wide veranda encircling the hotel.

As Barclay hoped, the hotel lured the wealthy who enjoyed 'the country' in elegant style. The amenities offered by the hotel, among them the fine cuisine by a French chef, outweighed the difficulties of traveling to the remote village. In the beginning, visitors took the train to Glendale and then transferred to the stage for the remainder of the trip to the hotel. Later, long after Barclay lost the hotel, they arrived in fashionable Model T's, to the delight of local children.

Whether because of the exaggerated advertising, the promises of free barbecues and beer busts, or the luxurious hotel, crowds of people flocked to the Monte Vista Hotel

THE MONTE VISTA HOTEL

A COUNTRY HOTEL BILL OF FARE

SOUP

Oyster   Vegetable

HORS D'OEUVRES

Sliced Cucumbers   Sliced Tomatoes

SMALL PATTIES

Fish   Baked Salmon   Potatoes Hollandaise

REMOVES

Roast Sirloin of Beef, Brown Gravy

Roast Spring Chicken, Fresh Green Peas

Roast Saddle of Veal with Dressing

SALAD

Lettuce   Lobster

Potato   Shrimp

ENTREES

Stewed Eggs, Alsatian Sauce   Mushrooms

French Pancake with Jelly   Asparagus on Toast

VEGETABLES

Mashed Irish Potatoes   Boiled Sweet Potatoes

Summer Squash   Fresh Green Peas

Stewed Tomatoes

DESSERT

Stewed Fruit Pudding, Brandy Sauce

Lemon Pie   Apple Pie   Raspberry Pie

Vanilla Ice Cream   Lemon Ice Cream

Assorted Cookies

Fruit   Crackers   Cheese

on weekends. From the observatory tower on the third floor of the hotel, Barclay showed perspective buyers a bird's-eye view of the land and pointed out general locations of plots for sale. Many bought un-surveyed and un-staked plots from that tower without taking the time to check specific locations. Barclay simply marked the sales on a map. Unfortunately for the buyers, Barclay failed to officially record the map or the deeds he gave to them, and lawsuits resulted for the next 20 years. Other settlers often quitclaimed[12] the land that buyers could not identify.

Barclay himself lived at the hotel with his wife and three daughters: Anna, Edith, and Mary. Anna earned a reputation in the village as an energetic tomboy. She married and remained in the area as Mrs. Kirby, known for her interest in studying foreign languages.

Mary met a tragic fate at age 20. After sharing an evening with friends in Burbank, she started home about 5:00 a.m. the next morning, dropped off a friend, and continued the journey alone in her horse-drawn carriage. At 8:20, midway between Roscoe and Monte Vista, a mail carrier found her body with her head wedged between a shaft and wheel of the carriage. Miss Phillips extricated the body, put the dead woman in the carriage, and brought Mary on her last journey home. The coroner's inquest ruled that Mary had apparently suffered from one of her epileptic seizures on the way home and had fallen head-

A side view of the Monte Vista taken years later shows the hotel had lost its tower, but trees and vines softened the landscape.
Photo courtesy of Bolton Hall Museum.

first between the shaft and the wheel. Unwittingly, the horse continued a few paces, fracturing her skull and "crushing her life out"[13] with a few revolutions of the wheel. Without a guiding hand, the horse finally stopped and waited patiently until Phillips found them.

What happened to other members of the family is unknown.

Barclay went bankrupt in 1888 with the demise of the land boom and lost the hotel. Dr. Quintin Rowley, brother of town leader Loron Rowley, bought it as an investment. The elegant hotel enjoyed years of popularity with sportsmen hunting in nearby canyons, with families vacationing in clean country air, and as a retreat for Los

Angles businessmen. It even had its scandals. "In 1908 a district attorney from Los Angles got caught with a woman at that hotel and it caused quite a ruckus," recalled an original settler, Paul Lancaster.[14]

The luxurious resort began its swan song during the First World War. In 1920 the Council of Community Service of the State of California bought the hotel to convert it to a home for undernourished children in Los Angeles County. The announcement in the *Glendale Evening News*, December 20, 1920, ran with emotional appeal for "future citizens of the republic, (who) will be fostered and cherished and brought to the full physical development that is their birthright." Community leaders John Steven McGroarty and M.V. Hartranft agreed to pay

The removal of the third story, the mansard roof, and the gingerbread woodwork ruined any historical value of the old hotel.
Photo courtesy of Bolton Hall Museum.

$500 for necessary repair work. "All the Boy Scouts of the county will be privileged to take charge of the clearing up and beautifying of the grounds."

The hotel as Cyprus Manor. Trees and weeds grew taller as the stature of the hotel dwindled. Photo courtesy of Bolton Hall Museum.

Mrs. R.W. Meeker of Glendale chaired efforts to furnish the kitchen, asking clubs and organizations to "…give just one good, aluminum utensil … for anything that benefits future citizens of our country should concern every patriotic citizen of the land, and claim his aid as far as he is able to give it." Despite all the emotional appeal, the home was not a success and closed its doors.

In 1923, the Volunteers of America refurbished the inside of the building as a home for the elderly and replaced the original wood foundation with stone. The next year, they 'modified' the outside by tearing down the top story, building a veranda around the second story, adding French doors from the rooms onto the veranda, and refinishing the outside walls with stucco.

The remodeling, especially the removal of the third story, the mansard roof, and the gingerbread woodwork, eliminated the features typical of Victorian architecture. Although the old hotel would continue to function as a rest home for many years, the "green monstrosity ... (now had) very little worth saving from an historical standpoint."[15]

The history of the last years of the hotel is sketchy. In 1948, the Volunteers of America celebrated the 25th anniversary of their rest home. In 1950, Harry Morrill, a

When the bulldozers arrived, only vandals and children stepped through the doorways of the 'haunted house.'
Photo from The Record-Ledger, April 9, 1964.

local builder, bought the home with the intention of making it a 'club house' for civic and service organizations with meeting rooms, a banquet hall, and recreational facilities. This apparently did not happen. In 1954, Mr. and Mrs. Robert Christopher bought the building, repainted and repaired it, and opened the Cypress Manor rest home, which closed in 1959.

Ruin replaced Victorian splendor. Vandals visited the once grand hotel, smashing windows, writing on walls, and strewing broken bottles across the floors. Neighbors, fearful for the safety of children investigating the 'haunted house,' petitioned for its destruction. In 1964 demolition crews moved in. "…the old building, constructed of grade A lumber, all center cut and without a single knot hole, stayed erect as long as possible against the bulldozer's relentless onslaughts."[16] Eventually, of course, the bulldozer won, crushing it and several other neighboring structures between Sherman Grove and Floralita. In the cleared area rose houses and apartment buildings.

#####

Original Maps for Monte Vista

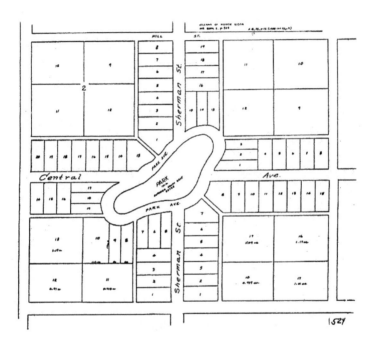

Plat Map 1

This plat map is thought to be the first design of the village by the original promoters, Sherman Page and F.C. Howes.

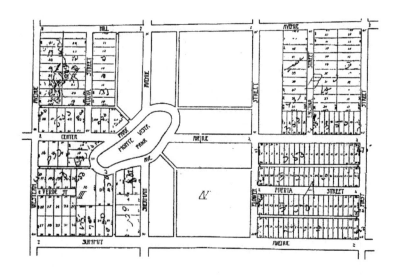

Plat Map 2

This revised plat map was mostly likely Frank Barclay's plan, after he bought the land from Page and Howes. Prices ranged from $300 to $650 per lot. Note that some sections are not divided into lots, indicating the land was not for sale.

Footnotes

[1] Cleland, Robert Glass, *From Wilderness to Empire: A History of California 1542-1900*. New York: Alfred A. Knopf, 1944, p. 357.

[2] Advertisement, *Los Angeles Daily Herald*, June 6, 1887.

[3] Advertisement, *Los Angeles Times*, Friday, July 1, 1887.

[4] John Joseph Johnson: born November 4, 1862 – died February 7, 1933.

[5] A legal document that belonged to Frank Barclay mentions the date June 19, 1886, as the date of "… the Abstract … relating to that portion of the Rancho Tujunga conveyed by F.C. Howes and Sherman Page to F.H. Barclay, et al. by deed …"

[6] Advertisement, *Los Angeles Times*, Friday, July 1, 1887.

[7] "Six Persons Owned Valley When Anna Jump Arrived," *The Record-Ledger*, Thursday, September 30, 1954, A-4.

[8] Advertisement, *Los Angeles Times*, Friday, July 1, 1887.

[9] Ibid.

[10] Some sources claim the hotel cost $20,000 to build; others claim $30,000.

[11] Advertisement, *Los Angeles Times*, Friday, July 1, 1887.

[12] Quitclaim: to release a legal claim, especially on a parcel of real estate, without a warranty of title. In this case, since owners could not identify their parcels of land, others who settled on the land claimed it since the owners "quit" it.

[13] "Killed on the Road," Clippings file, Bolton Hall Museum.

[14] "He Was Here in the Beginning," *The Record-Ledger*, February 12, 1986.

[15] "Cypress Manor Passes into Oblivion," *The Record-Ledger*, April 9, 1964.

[16] Ibid.

Bibliography

Advertisement. *Los Angeles Daily Herald*, June 6, 1887.

Advertisement. *Los Angeles Times*, Friday, July 1, 1887.

Advertisement. *Los Angeles Times*, Sunday, July 3, 1887.

Advertisement. November 1885. Clippings file, Bolton Hall Museum.

Advertisement. *Rural Californian*, November 1884.

Advertisement. *Rural Californian*, November 1885.

"Advertisement in LA Times Dated 1887 Boasts Marvels of Monte Vista: Los Angeles Times, Friday, July 1, 1887." *The Record-Ledger*, September 27, 1973.

"Anna Kirby's Father Built Community's First Hotel." *The Record-Ledger*, September 30, 1954.

Austin, Lee. "Hostelry Built in 1887 Soon to Be Demolished." *Los Angeles Times*, Sunday, January 12, 1964.

Barclay, Frank H. Copies of personal papers and legal documents.

Boales, Jane. "Recalling Old Monte Vista Hotels." *The Record-Ledger*, October 20, 1979.

"Born at Old Monte Vista Hotel Speaker Revives Past of Area." *The Record-Ledger*, Thursday, February 11, 1974, p. 11.

Carlson, Viola. "Monte Vista Park Hotel: Oldest Building in Sunland-Tujunga." 1968.

Cleland, Robert Glass. *The Cattle on a Thousand Hills: Southern California, 1850-1880.* San Marino, CA: The Huntington Library. 1951.

Cleland, Robert Glass. *From Wilderness to Empire: A History of California, 1542-1900*. New York: Alfred A. Knopf. 1944.

"Cypress Manor Passes into Oblivion." *The Record-Ledger*, April 9, 1964.

Dumpke, Glenn S. *The Boom of the Eighties in Southern California*. San Marino, CA: Huntington Library. 1991.

Egremont, Angela. "Monte Vista Hotel: Important to Sunland-Tujunga Past." *The Leader*, Wednesday, August 30, 1989. p. 5."1880s – Boom and Bust Days in Southland." *Daily News*, date unknown.

Green Verdugo Hills: A Chronicle of Sunland-Tujunga, Calif. and How It Grew. Tujunga, CA: The Record-Ledger of the Verdugo Hills.

Harn, Jay. "He Was Here in the Beginning." *The Record-Ledger*, February 12, 1986.

Hartranft, M.V. "Monte Vista Park." *The Western Empire Land-Banking and Home Securing Plan*. January, 1911.

"Historic Hotel May Become Hub of Civic Life." *Glendale NewsPress*, Wednesday, April 19, 1950.

Hitt, Marlene. "Everyone Invited to Visit the Monte Vista Park Hotel." *Foothill Leader*, June 13, 1998.

"Hunting Lodge for Wealthy of 1870s on Skids." (sic) *Los Angeles Times*, September 10, 1961.

"Killed on the Road." Clippings file, Bolton Hall Museum.

"Landmark Ruined." *The Record-Ledger*, Sunday, February 14, 1971.

Little Landers Historical Society. *Docent Handbook*. Bolton Hall Museum.

"Los Angeles and the Land Boom of the 1880s." *Network: Los Angeles Network for Education in Local and California History*. June 1984. Vol. 3, No. 4.

McWilliams, Carey. *Southern California: An Island on the Land*. Salt Lake City: Peregrine Smith Books. 1973.

Miller, Charles. "Sunland-Tujunga's Ties to Hollywood." *Foothill Leader*, September 7, 1988.

"Monte Vista Hotel: Important to Sunland-Tujunga's Past." *The Leader*, Wednesday, August 30, 1989. p. 5.

"Monte Vista Hotel 1887 Country Hotel Bill of Fare." Bolton Hall Museum.

"Old Building to Look Like New." *The Record-Ledger*, October 16, 1924.

"Old Jump Home Open to Tours During S-T Old Timers Week." *The Record-Ledger*, August 8, 1968.

Page, Sherman. "Monte Vista." Henry E. Huntington Library, Pasadena, California.

Plat maps of Monte Vista. Bolton Hall Museum.

"Refitting Monte Vista Lodge for New Purpose." *The Record-Ledger*, November 22, 1923.

"Rowley Recalls Early Days of Sunland-Tujunga." *The Record-Ledger*, Thursday, September 27, 1973.

Rowley, Robert. Personal interview by Viola Carlson. 1974.

"Saga of Monte Vista." *The Record-Ledger*, Thursday, June 18, 1964.

"Six Persons Owned Valley When Anna Jump Arrived." *The Record-Ledger*, Thursday, September 30, 1954. A-4.

"Son of Late William C. Graham Recalls Coming to Sunland in 1909 with Father." *The Record-Ledger*, September 30, 1954. A-3.

"Starting Semi-Weekly Dances at Monte Vista Inn." *The Record-Ledger*, May 24, 1923.

"Story of One Little Wire and How It Grew." *The Record-Ledger*, Historical & Progress Edition, May 21, 1953.

"Sunland First Developed in Big 1887 Land Boom." *The Record-Ledger*, September 12, 1968.

Sunland-Tujunga: Nestled between the Verdugo Hills and the San Gabriel Mts. The Sunland-Tujunga Chamber of Commerce. March 1947.

"Telephone Company Office." *The Record-Ledger*, Thursday, July 28, 1955.

"This Is the Hotel that Was." *The Record-Ledger*, April 8, 1964.

"To Open Home for Aged at Sunland." *The Record-Ledger*, Thursday, December 13, 1923.

"Tujunga, 'Home of Health' Has Many Sanitariums, Rest Homes for Aged." *The Record-Ledger*, Thursday, August 16, 1956.

"Volunteers of America, Sunland Guest Home to Have Children." *The Record-Ledger*, Thursday, August 19, 1948.

The Roscoe Robbers
and the Sensational
Train Wrecking of 1894

**"...the boldest train robbery that ever
took place in Southern California..."**

The Early History of Sunland, California
Volume 2

ML Tiernan

Two robbers posed as passengers to flag down the train. When the engineer recognized danger, he opened the throttle and sped past. The bandits threw the spur switch, and the train careened full speed off the tracks.

The Roscoe Robbers

and the Sensational
Train Wrecking of 1894

*Greed and dastardly deeds shake the
quiet little village of Sunland.*

**The Early History of Sunland, California
Volume 2**

ML Tiernan

The Roscoe Robbers

and the Sensational Train Wrecking of 1894

www.maryleetiernan.com

Second printing April 1, 2015

10 9 8 7 6 5 4 3 2

ISBN 978-0983067214 (Paperback)

Photographs on cover courtesy of Bolton Hall Museum, Tujunga, California.

Quote on cover from "Looted the Express Car," *San Francisco Examiner*, February 17, 1894, Part 1, p.1.

Contents

Foreword

In 1876, the Southern Pacific Railroad finished the line connecting Los Angeles to San Francisco. That line also joined with the continental railroad and opened Southern California for settlement. Speculators spied the opportunity to make fortunes by duping a gullible public and rushed about promoting land deals. People from all over the nation, and even from Europe, poured into the 'promised land.' Some cities, like Glendale and Pasadena, thrived during this land boom of the 1880s. Others, like the little village of Monte Vista, did not fare as well. In fact, because of the failure to populate the village, history catalogs Monte Vista as a "ghost town."

From the east:

Monte Vista was not easily accessible because of its location. Dusty roads wound their way north from Glendale into the foothills, then west across the valley along Horsethief Trail. Woodcutters, gold prospectors, and homesteaders trekked across the valley on the trail, which allegedly began as a footpath for Spanish padres travelling between the San Gabriel and San Fernando Missions. The mountainous terrain with its numerous wooded canyons en route also offered a safe haven for horse thieves and other outlaws, which explains the trail's name. Part of this trail later became Honolulu Avenue.

From the west:

Access to the valley improved greatly with the opening of a route on the western end of town for passengers arriving by train. The Southern Pacific Railroad ran a steam train out of downtown Los Angeles into the San Fernando Valley, stopping at the tiny Roscoe Depot. A horse and buggy ride completed the four-and-a-half-mile trip into Monte Vista via Roscoe Blvd. Heartier adventurers sometimes walked the rough, pitted road to the village.

By 1886, about two dozen people had settled in Monte Vista with about 250 acres of land under irrigation. Although the train delivered mail as early as 1885, the post office wasn't officially established until 1887. The opening of the post office, however, created a problem. Since a post office named Monta Vista already existed, the postmaster refused to approve another with so similar a name. Thus Monte Vista became Sunland.

By the mid-1890s, Sunland remained a small village of farmers and ranchers. Trains whisked passengers and Wells Fargo bank shipments from Los Angeles to San Francisco past the tiny depot of Roscoe. The train only stopped at Roscoe when signaled to do so.

First Attempt

A little after 10:30 p.m. on December 23, 1893, the northbound Southern Pacific Train #20 left Arcade Station in Los Angeles on its regular run through the San Fernando Valley to San Francisco. Most passengers probably boarded #20 late that Saturday night preoccupied with thoughts of Christmas and their families. At least one passenger, however, embarked with a more sinister goal when the train stopped briefly at Burbank.

According to one dramatic version, a constable at the depot grabbed four tramps attempting to climb aboard a baggage car. One of them, a young man dressed in a black slouch hat and overcoat, wrestled himself free of the constable's grasp. Running down the tracks, with the constable in hot pursuit, the young man vaulted onto the train just as it left the station.

In a less theatrical version, the constable at Burbank noted two passengers exiting the last coach at the rear of the train. Because they wore dark clothing, they quickly blended into the night, and the constable paid no more attention to them. Apparently, though, one of them used the cover of darkness to backtrack to the train and climb up the 'blind end' of the baggage or express car. During the next four miles, as the train climbed the uphill grade, he worked his way toward the front of the train.

A flare from his confederate waiting at Roscoe depot signaled the bandit. He jumped down into the coal tender, sinking up to his knees in coal. In true Old West fashion, a mask obscured his face and a six-shooter jutted from each hand. He punctuated his command to the engineer to stop the train by firing into the cab.

As the engineer set the brakes and the train screeched to a standstill, the second, older masked man, carrying a Winchester rifle, emerged from the darkness. At gunpoint, the younger bandit forced the engineer and fireman out of the cab.

Meanwhile, the shots and the cessation of movement alerted other trainmen to trouble. One of the postal clerks poked his head out the door. Spotting the robbers steering the engineer and fireman toward the express car, he ducked back inside and warned his cohorts to keep quiet. Trainmen were well aware that nervous holdup men usually answered resistance by shooting those who interfered.

The gunshots also prompted a constable, traveling as a passenger, to investigate. But when the robbers blandished their guns in his face and told him to "get," he quickly scrambled back inside the coach. Not wanting any more interference, the robbers shot several warning shots as they walked along the side of the train and yelled for passengers and trainmen alike to stay inside and not meddle.

These gunmen followed the typical pattern of most train robberies, first, by their method of stopping the train, and secondly, by leaving the passengers alone. Since trains transported fortunes in valuables and money, the potential booty in the express and postal cars far outweighed what little the passengers might be carrying. The chance of easy wealth tempted the unsuccessful and the lazy—or those who wanted to get back at the railroad. Hatred of the railroad encouraged holdups; many regarded the robbers as folk heroes, helping them to hide and escape.

The two captives, knowing a twitchy finger meant death, complied with the gunmen's directions. Finally the express car loomed before them. The bandits demanded that the messenger open the door. When he did not respond, they blew it apart with dynamite. Confronted by the gunmen, the dazed guard inside the car opened the safe and handed over its contents—about $150.

Disappointed and worried about a clean getaway, the bandits demanded the engineer drive the train off the side track and derail it. The pleas of the engineer persuaded them to change their minds. Instead, the engineer and fireman promised to walk down the track and wait for a signal to return to the cab. This they did, while the bandits disappeared into the night on horseback. A short time later a distant shot rang out.

By the time the train resumed its journey and reached the next station in San Fernando where trainmen notified the authorities, several hours had elapsed. So it wasn't until about 4:00 a.m. that Detective Will Smith of the Southern Pacific could round up a posse. When the posse reached Roscoe, they found the tracks of two men and two horses, but rain obliterated the trail into the sparsely populated mountains. To make matters worse, no one could clearly describe the robbers. The dim light at the lonely little depot obscured their faces as effectively as their masks. Had the robbers left well enough alone, they would never have been discovered.

Try Again

Seven weeks later the bandits tried again, with far more serious consequences. As Train #20 chugged along the upgrade to Roscoe on Thursday, February 15, 1894, bright moonlight revealed two men waiting at the tiny depot. The engineer, David W. Thomas, groaned inwardly at the thought of stopping, with the train already behind schedule, for only two passengers. Suddenly, one of figures jumped up, lit a torch, and started waving it in one hand—a signal to stop the train. But Thomas also saw the man's other hand—clenching a rifle. Instantaneously, Thomas recalled the previous robbery at this same depot and knew he was dealing with bandits, not passengers.

Instead of slowing, Thomas hoped to avoid confrontation by opening the throttle and speeding past. The bandits, however, had broken the switch lock and thrown the spur switch, and the train careened full speed onto the blind siding. One robber yelled, "Stop! Stop her!" and fired into the cab as the train rushed by. Thomas's efforts to slow the train on the short track failed.

The locomotive plowed over the ties at the end of the

track, pulling two freight cars filled with oranges off the track with it. Like an animal trying to burrow into the ground, as the locomotive hit the soft, sandy ground, it ploughed into the earth creating a ditch about five feet deep. The impact finally stopped the train about 20 feet past the end of the track. The freight cars crashed into one another and slammed into the locomotive.

Thomas and Benjamin LeGrande, an off-duty fireman hitching a ride to San Fernando, managed to jump to safety, but fireman Arthur Masters lost his footing as the locomotive thumped over the ground. The final impact pinned him against the locomotive's blazing hot boiler, crushing his legs and guaranteeing a living hell. The collision also caught two tramps, Harry Dailey[1] and James Pacey, riding on the cowcatcher. The jolt threw Pacey 50 feet and rendered him unconscious for 15 to 20 minutes. The left cylinder crushed the 19-year-old Dailey.

Thomas ran for cover behind a cactus bush fearful that the robbers would shoot him for not stopping the train. He remained hidden, with a sprained wrist, while screams of agony from Masters sent LeGrande running to the passenger car to get help. Unfortunately, he ran straight into the bandits. Ignoring Masters's cries of anguish, the robbers waylaid LeGrande from his errand of mercy and compelled him to accompany them to the Wells Fargo car to assist in dynamiting the door.

The explosion rocked the night and lit the sky. The blast splintered the door and damaged the frame all around it. When the smoke cleared, the robbers forced the fireman to join the express messenger, Edgar, inside the car. As Edgar opened the safe, sacks of booty revealed themselves. The younger robber then stood guard at the door, firing randomly to dissuade anyone from thinking about interfering, while the older one grabbed the bags of gold and silver from the safe and shoved them into a large gunny sack.

After the bandits drove off into the night, LeGrande and Edgar ran back to the locomotive to rescue Masters. For the next hour, while they and others, including the recovered Pacey, worked to free him, Masters pleaded in agony that they stop his intolerable suffering and kill him or give him a gun so he could do it himself. They finally loosened the beam that trapped him, minutes after Masters died.

The Roscoe Train Depot

This tiny, isolated depot became the gateway to Sunland from the west. Because passengers signaled the train when they wanted to board, Roscoe was referred to as a "flag stop." The building no longer exists, but the site of the depot would now be in Sun Valley, California. Photo courtesy of the Union Pacific Museum Collection, SP Collection.

The Investigation

Newspaper headlines screamed about the wreck and robbery. The *San Francisco Examiner* called it "…the boldest train robbery that ever took place in Southern California, or, for that matter, in the State."[2] The exact amount stolen from the train during the robbery will never be known since neither the Southern Pacific nor Wells Fargo would disclose a dollar value for the loss. Newspapers could only speculate, and given their tendency toward sensationalism, speculate they did. Some guessed the value as high as $100,000.

The practice of the railroad companies not to divulge dollar figures for robbery losses gave rise to another sort of speculation. In truth, based on later evidence, the Roscoe robbers only confiscated some gold and about $1200 in Mexican silver coins. But the tendency to exaggerate gave birth to tales of hidden treasure. If newspaper reported $20,000 or $50,000 or $100,000 had been stolen, where was the unrecovered loot? Adventurers dreamed of discovering lost wealth buried in haste by holdup men who never reclaimed their treasure. Robbers who could not find their hiding places after long terms in prison helped the growth of such legends.

The Roscoe robbery headlined in the news, however, not because of the amount of money stolen, but because of the train wrecking and the horrible deaths of Masters and Dailey. Wells Fargo and the Southern Pacific upped the usual $300 reward by Wells Fargo and $300 from the state by offering an additional $1,000 for the arrest and conviction of each robber. In spite of the extra incentive, lack of clues stymied investigators.

Popular theory held that as many as five men executed the robbery, but witnesses could describe only two of them: both with light complexions and blue eyes wearing dark overcoats, black slouch hats, and masks. Witnesses characterized their physical stature as one smaller, one larger; or one heavier, one slender; or one taller, one shorter. Actually their heights would turn out to be less than an inch different. Such general descriptions caused many a finger to point at the wrong men; indeed, four innocent men were arrested, but eventually released.

The first detectives on the scene, a posse headed by Sheriff Cline, followed a trail west from Roscoe for seven or eight miles toward Lankershim in the direction of Cahuenga Pass. Along the way, they found Wells Fargo tags, totaling about $800, removed from money sacks. Then the trail stopped, as did the tags, because once again, rain helped the robbers by wiping out their tracks. As with the first robbery, detectives would come to the conclusion that unless the robbers did something to give themselves away, they would probably not be caught.

Alva Johnson and his first wife Mary A. Phillippi to whom he was married at the time of the train robbery. Photo courtesy of Glen M. Johnson.

Shortly after the train robbery, John J. Johnson visited the county sheriff and implicated his thirty-six-year-old brother Alvarado (Alva) Johnson[3] and his ranch hands Kid (William H.) Thompson and George Smith in the train robbery and wrecking.

The Johnsons, one of the founding families in Sunland, had been feuding over water rights. Alva's father, Farmer A. Johnson, and his brother Cornelius ranched the land Farmer had homesteaded in the early 1880s in Big Tujunga Canyon. John, in addition to owning and running the Monte Vista Inn across from Sunland Park, homesteaded canyon land adjacent to his father's.

Alva's ranch lay downstream from the other Johnson ranches. Originally Alva worked on the ranch for Peter Phillippi. When the older German farmer died, Alva married his much younger widow, Mary.[4] The Phillippi ranch, now Alva's, depended on water from the canyon. When Farmer and John opened a water company by damming the water from the canyon, they cut off Alva's supply. Alva hired lawyers and filed lawsuits trying to open the flow of water. The costly processes breed animosity between father and son, and between brother and brother, and sent Alva deeper and deeper into debt.

According to John, his brother needed money to pay for these legal expenses. John claimed he saw Alva drive past his house heading for home in the very early morning hours after the robbery and rain. He also maintained that the getaway tracks matched those of a wagon and horse belonging to his brother, and that Alva fit the description of one of the robbers. Although John could not give any hard evidence against his brother, since investigators had few other leads, John's suspicions turned the investigation in Alva's direction.

Initially, detectives found that the thirty-six-year-old Alva was a respected rancher who raised cattle and poultry in Big Tujunga Canyon and operated a feed store at 226 Franklin Street near Broadway in Los Angeles. Although on friendly terms with his sister Olive and her husband George Trogdon, relations with his father and brothers John and Cornelius had deteriorated during the legal battles over rights to the stream waters in Big Tujunga Canyon.

The red-headed Johnson lived with his wife, Mary, and his two small children Jesse and Mathilda, and two stepdaughters Kate and Minnie. Alva hated the Southern Pacific, a sentiment not uncommon to ranchers and farmers who felt powerful railroad influence and fees controlled too much of their lives. What tweaked the detectives' curiosity were Alva's comments to neighbors blaming the train wreck on the engineer for not stopping.

Circumstantial evidence against Alva, Kid Thompson, and George Smith began to mount. A witness named

Degen swore he saw Kid Thompson on Train #20 the night of the first robbery and believed the Kid was the one who jumped into the locomotive with two drawn revolvers. Alva and the Kid fit the descriptions of the bandits and both owned clothes and guns similar to those of the robbers. When detectives began questioning Alva, Kid Thompson disappeared.

The wagon tracks proved the most damaging circumstantial evidence. Tracks found at the scene roughly matched those of Alva's wagon, odd tracks from a wagon with a worn axle. At the trial months later, Constable L.D. Rogers would conveniently claim he continued following the wagon tracks from where Sheriff Cline's posse left off. He said they led him to Glendale, then back up to Monte Vista Valley, past John Johnson's house to Alva's ranch.

Kid Thompson and George Smith, both of whom had criminal records, worked for Alva. By age 24, the Kid had already accumulated quite a history. Born in Colorado in 1871, he first came to California in July 1893. From October 1893 to March 1, 1894, he worked for Alva both at the ranch and at his store in Los Angeles. He apparently worked intermittently as a ranch hand, between planning robberies and serving time in prison. Several days after the robbery, George enjoyed a night at a "disreputable house" on Alameda Street, pleasures he paid for with gold.

The Arrest

Although they possessed no hard evidence, police hoped Alva would break if arrested since he was very nervous and agitated under questioning. And so Constable Rogers arrived at Alva's home on Sunday afternoon, March 25, 1894, to take him into custody. The evidence presented at the preliminary hearing on March 30 and 31 was weak and the charges dismissed.

The announcement brought a wave of applause from spectators while his wife and children embraced the freed man. General sentiment in the community favored Alva as innocent and condemned the Johnson family for turning against one of their own. Many felt Alva's father and brothers tried to railroad him out of animosity for losing the lawsuit in Superior Court over the water rights. Not long after, the father Farmer sold his property to his son Cornelius and moved to Bakersfield. His brother John became reclusive.

Alvarado (Alva) Johnson
Photo courtesy of the California State Archives

The Break

Investigation continued, by police, by the railroad, by Wells Fargo. Finally, in October, Charles Etzler reported a damning story to authorities. While tramping a train ride to Los Angeles, Etzler met Kid Thompson when the Kid climbed down from the roof of the car to join him. After being caught and thrown off the train, they walked to Alva's ranch where the Kid said he could get some money. On the way, the Kid bragged about the Roscoe robberies in detail.

Alva, upset at seeing the Kid, refused to give him any money unless he returned to Arizona. Alva feared the Kid would sell the Mexican coins to the Chinese in Los Angeles and the detectives would find out. The next day, the three drove to Los Angeles with the Kid hiding under the wagon seat covered with a blanket. On the way, both Alva and the Kid freely discussed the holdups.

According to Etzler, the Kid initiated the idea for the robbery and talked Alva into joining him. Gunmen in the Old West usually consisted of two types: those with a natural disrespect for the rights and property of others, and those who accepted the social order but could easily be turned to crime to settle grievances.[5] The Roscoe robbers fit each category: Kid Thompson, the career criminal, who planned one robbery after the other; and Alva Johnson, worried about his mortgage after lawsuits drained his finances, who targeted the railroad as a scapegoat for his problems.

The Kid returned to Arizona and several weeks later received a parcel at Tempe, Arizona, containing $600: 30 small packages of $20 each in Mexican money. Etzler helped the Kid launder the money in Phoenix through several Chinese shopkeepers who bought the coins for 40-45 cents on the dollar. Mexican silver, being purer than U.S. silver, was used as a trade coin in China. The Kid immediately began planning another robbery, but Etzler refused to join him and fled.

With Etzler's testimony, the police arrested Alva. The story also persuaded George Smith to admit that Alva and the Kid were not on the ranch the night of the robbery, but came home early the next morning. Meanwhile authorities in Arizona also caught and arrested the Kid.

The U.S. Marshall had warned cowboys to be on the lookout for Thompson and a companion, a 17-year-old named Tupper. Hearing they had been sighted nearby, Deputy Sheriff Billy Moore formed a posse which spotted the Kid and his companion and gave chase. The posse overtook them around dark in the Four Peak Range. Cornered, but refusing to surrender, the Kid and Tupper abandoned their horses and retreated into a rocky canyon. They began shooting at the posse from the shelter of an overhanging cliff. Shots rang back and forth for hours until the freezing night air forced the outlaws to surrender.

After Thompson was escorted back to Los Angeles, the State charged both he and Johnson: "…did willfully, unlawfully and feloniously throw out a switch at Roscoe Station on the railroad known as Southern Pacific, with the intention then and there of derailing a passenger train, and did then and there willfully, unlawfully and feloniously board a passenger train on said railroad at said station with the intention there and then of robbing the said passenger train."[6] The deaths of Masters and Dailey raised the felony to a capital offense crime. Face to face with the Kid in the same jail, Alva realized both of them might hang.

William H. (Kid) Thompson
Photo courtesy of the California State Archives

The Verdict

Alva realized that pleading guilty could save his life by commuting his sentence to life imprisonment. Afraid of dying and pressured by his wife Mary and sister Olive to save his neck, Alva confessed and agreed to testify against the Kid. Johnson testified that he and the Kid drove to Roscoe on February 15th. They reached the depot about sundown, feed the horses, and waited at the switch. Johnson accused the Kid of throwing the spur switch, but subsequently, the Kid would accuse Johnson of doing the same. The argument would later save Thompson's neck.

After the robbery, they drove back to L.A. disguising the wagon as a milk wagon by covering it with canvas. On the way, they met four or five policemen who stopped them, but allowed them to pass after warning them about the robbers. Later, they returned to Johnson's ranch and buried the money in the orchard. When the Kid decided to leave town, they divided only the gold. The Kid returned about eight months later wanting his share of the silver, but Johnson feared Thompson's erratic character would get them into trouble and insisted the Kid return to Arizona.

He sent him $600 via Wells Fargo express to Tempe under the name W.S. Parker.

During the confession, Alva conceded that he based part of his decision to confess on his desire to save the ranch for his wife and children; attorneys wanted the ranch as payment for their fees to defend him. He also disclosed the location of $576 in Mexican silver hidden on the ranch. During sentencing on November 17, 1895, Alva sobbed uncontrollably until the judge announced a life sentence at the state prison at San Quentin because he had saved the county the expense of a trial.

A jury found Kid Thompson guilty as charged on May 8, 1895. A week later, Judge Bill Smith of the Superior Court sentenced Thompson to San Quentin to be hanged on July 19 between 10:00 a.m. and 4:00 p.m.

"Two men were killed, the fireman especially suffering the most excruciating torture for over an hour. Yet you, knowing him to be in that awful situation, suffering those tortures, at the same time went about the robbery, indifferent to his cries and appeals for relief. The laws of California provide that when a man does these things he may suffer the penalty of death; at least, imprisonment for life, and it is a very just law."[7]

The Aftermath

Fortunately for Thompson, his lawyer Ben Goodrich, took advantage of poorly written statues regarding train robberies. The lawyer managed to overturn the conviction on appeal. He argued that Thompson had been convicted on the basis of throwing the spur switch to cause the derailment of the train, yet no one had proved he had done so. Therefore, he could only be punished for robbing the express car.[8] Thompson was retried in April 1897 and convicted with a life sentence in Folsom.

Alva attempted to escape from San Quentin on July 19, 1900. He managed to scale the wall and slip into darkness when a patrol guard spotted Alva's partner. The guard fired, killing the second prisoner. Hearing the shots, Alva knew there was little hope of getting away. He ran anyway, but quickly tired and guards easily caught up with him. Shortly thereafter, Mary Johnson filed for a divorce which was granted by default on October 12, 1900, because Alva failed to appear in court. Seven years passed. Finally, through the efforts of parents and friends, Alva was paroled on October 21, 1907.

Alva and his second wife Catherine
in Modesto, CA.
Photo courtesy of Glen M. Johnson.

After Alva's release, he moved north to Bakersfield to live with his father Farmer. In 1909, at age 51, he appealed for a full pardon. On his Application for Executive Clemency, when asked for reasons why he should be considered for a pardon, he wrote, "I have been out on parole since October 21st, 1907. I have been honest and have been during that time working and following honest occupations. I wish to get married and go to Ellensburg, Washington. I am to be married there."[9] The request for a pardon was granted on November 14, 1909, and became effective on March 25, 1910.

Ten years later, Alva lived in California with his wife Catherine as a dairyman in the town of Oakdale. Apparently years had mended the family rift. Alva and his brother John were driving together in Sacramento on September 6, 1920, when a street car ran into John's automobile. The impact threw Alva from the automobile and fractured his skull. He died three days later in the hospital on September 9 at age 63.

#####

Map of Sunland in the 1890s

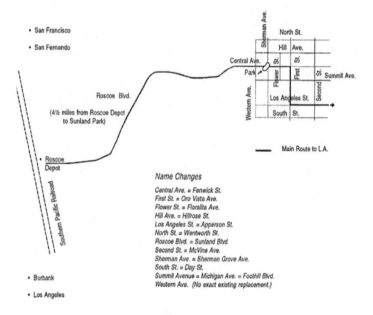

- San Francisco
- San Fernando

Sherman Ave.

North St.

Hill Ave.

Central Ave.

Park

Flower St.

First St.

Second St.

Summit Ave.

Western Ave.

Los Angeles St.

South St.

Roscoe Blvd.

(4½ miles from Roscoe Depot to Sunland Park)

Main Route to L.A.

- Roscoe Depot

Southern Pacific Railroad

Name Changes

Central Ave. = Fenwick St.
First St. = Oro Vista Ave.
Flower St. = Floralita Ave.
Hill Ave. = Hillrose St.
Los Angeles St. = Apperson St.
North St. = Wentworth St.
Roscoe Blvd. = Sunland Blvd.
Second St. = McVine Ave.
Sherman Ave. = Sherman Grove Ave.
South St. = Day St.
Summit Avenue = Michigan Ave. = Foothill Blvd.
Western Ave. (No exact existing replacement.)

- Burbank
- Los Angeles

Footnotes

[1] Newspapers tagged the young man with so many different names that it is difficult to ascertain which one is correct. The name Harry Dailey is used here because that name was reported in the account where his brother identified the body.

[2] "Looted the Express Car," *San Francisco Examiner,* February 17, 1894, p. 1.

[3] Alvarado (Alva) Johnson: born August 23, 1858 – died September 9, 1920.

[4] Alva Johnson and Mary A. Phillippi married on March 7, 1887.

[5] Block, Eugene B., *Great Train Robberies of the West*, New York: Coward-McCann, Inc., 1959.

[6] People vs. Alva Johnson and W.H. Thompson. Justice's Court, County of Los Angeles, State of California, October 23, 1894. County Records Center, Los Angeles, CA.

[7] "Must Suffer Death," Clippings file, Wells Fargo Historical Services.

[8] Patterson, Richard, *The Train Robbery Era: An Encyclopedic History*, Boulder, Colorado: Pruett Publishing Company, 1991, p. 239.

[9] Application for Pardon / Executive Clemency, #7778, from San Quentin, September 15, 1909. California State Archives, Sacramento.

Bibliography

"Affecting Scenes in Court." *San Francisco Examiner*, Sunday, April 1, 1984.

"Alva Johnson." *Los Angeles Herald*, Thursday, April 15, 1897.

"Big Reward for the Train Robbers." *Pasadena Daily Evening Star*, Saturday, February 17, 1894.

Block, Eugene B. *Great Train Robberies of the West*. New York: Coward-McCann, Inc. 1959.

Boessenecker, John. *Badge and Buckshot: Lawlessness in Old California*. Norman and London: University of Oklahoma Press, 1987. pp. 178-179.

Breakenridge, William M. *Helldorado: Bringing the Law to the Mesquite*. Glorieta, NM: The Rio Grande Press. 1970. pp. 231-235.

"Caught by Cowboys." Clippings file, Wells Fargo Historical Services.

"Charged with Train Robbery." *Los Angeles Herald*, Tuesday, March 27, 1894.

"Death the Penalty." Clippings file, Wells Fargo Historical Services.

"He Testified." *Los Angeles Herald*, Friday, April 16, 1897.

"Held to Answer." *The Los Angeles Sunday Times*, Sunday, November 18, 1894.

"Horsethief Trail Probably Used By Outlaws During Early Raids." *The Record-Ledger*, Historical & Progress Edition, May 21, 1953.

"In a Bank Robbery." Clippings file, Wells Fargo Historical Services.

"Johnson Tells All." *San Francisco Chronicle*, Sunday, May 5, 1895.

"Left No Tracks." *The Los Angeles Times*, Sunday, February 18, 1894.

"Looted the Express Car." *San Francisco Examiner,* Saturday, February 17, 1894.

"Man Hit by Street Car Dies of Broken Skull." *Sacramento Bee,* Thursday, September 9, 1920.

"Must Suffer Death." Clippings file, Wells Fargo Historical Services.

"Not Yet Captured." *The Los Angeles Times*, Tuesday, December 26, 1893.

"Not the Robbers." *Pasadena Daily Evening Star*, Saturday, March 31, 1894.

"Only Two Men Seen." *The Los Angeles Times*, Monday, December 25, 1893.

Patterson, Richard. *The Train Robbery Era: An Encyclopedic History*, Boulder, Colorado: Pruett Publishing Company, 1991.

Perry, Caswell E. and Parcher, Carroll W. *Glendale Area History*. Glendale, CA: Eric Schneirsohn. 1947. pp. 143, 146-148.

Pinkerton, William Allan. *Train Robberies, Train Robbers, and the "Holdup" Men*. New York: Arno Press, 1974.

"Roscoe Again." *The Los Angeles Times*, Friday, February 16, 1894.

"Roscoe Robbers." *The Los Angeles Times*, Saturday, February 17, 1894.

"Sentenced for Life." *San Francisco Examiner*, Sunday, December 16, 1894.

"Sheriff Cline Arrests Four Suspected Train Robbers." *Pasadena Daily Evening Star*, Saturday, February 17, 1894.

"State's Evidence." *The Los Angeles Times*, Sunday, October 21, 1894.

"Still in the Dark." *The Los Angeles Times*, Wednesday, February 21, 1894.

"The S.P. Train Robbery." *Pasadena Daily Evening Star*, Friday, February 16, 1894.

"Two Men Arrested for the Roscoe Train Robbery." *Pasadena Daily Evening Star*, Monday, March 26, 1894.

"Veiled in Mystery." *The Los Angeles Times*, Monday, February 19, 1894.

Documents:

Application for Pardon / Executive Clemency, #7778, from San Quentin, September 15, 1909. California State Archives, Sacramento.

Extraction from map book dated 1906. Bolton Hall Museum.

File #35267 in the Superior Court, County of Los Angeles, State of California. Mary A. Johnson, Plaintiff vs. Alva Johnson, Defendant. (Divorce papers.) August 2, 1900.

Folsom Prison Register, MFI:9(2). 1896-1910. California State Archives, Sacramento.

Letter from J.A. Fillmore, Southern Pacific Company to U.S. Marshalls, Sheriffs and Constables, February 16, 1894. Wells Fargo Historical Services.

Letter of intent to file for a pardon from Alva Johnson to J.D. Fredericks, District Attorney, Los Angeles. March 15, 1910. California State Archives, Sacramento.

Letter of recommendation for executive clemency from the State Board of Prison Directors, San Quentin. November 14, 1909. California State Archives, Sacramento.

Marriage License, State of California, County of Los Angeles between Alva Johnson and Mary A. Phillippi. March 16, 1887.

People vs. Alva Johnson and W.H. Thompson. Justice's Court, County of Los Angeles, State of California, October 23, 1894. County Records Center, Los Angeles, CA.

People vs. Alva Johnson and W.H. Thompson. Justice's Court, County of Los Angeles, State of California, November 12, 1894. County Records Center, Los Angeles, CA.

People vs. W.H. Thompson. Superior Court, County of Los Angeles, State of California, May 23, 1895. County Records Center, Los Angeles, CA.

Plat Map of Monte Vista Park Tract circa 1884. Bolton Hall Museum.

San Quentin Prison Register, MFI:9(12). 1882-1897. California State Archives, Sacramento.

The Parson and His Cemetery

**"Lord, I'm Coming Home...
Never More to Roam"**

The Early History of Sunland, California
Volume 3

ML Tiernan

Parson Wornum was so loved that when he died, the whole village attended his funeral. Years of neglect of his cemetery spelled disaster in 1978 when heavy rains tore open graves and washed bodies down the hillside.

The Parson
and His Cemetery

Parson Wornum and his wife Jenny ride
into Sunland and into the hearts
of an entire community.

The Early History of Sunland, California
Volume 3

ML Tiernan

The Parson and His Cemetery

www.maryleetiernan.com
Second printing April 1, 2015
10 9 8 7 6 5 4 3 2

ISBN 978-0983067221 (Paperback)

Photographs on cover courtesy of Bolton Hall Museum,
Tujunga, California.
Quote on cover is the title of an old hymn.

Contents

The Parson Arrives

Parson Wornum and Aunt Jenny won the hearts
of an entire community.
Photo courtesy of Bolton Hall Museum.

Restless sleepers turned on their cots in the hot night air. Being outside under the stars, instead of inside hot stuffy houses, eased the difficulty of sleeping in the oppressive summer heat only slightly. Many a head was lifted from a pillow at the faint but distinct sound of horses' hooves clopping down the dirt road. Could that be…? Then a strong, familiar voice reverberated across the valley singing the old hymn "Lord, I'm Coming Home—Never More to Roam."[1] Lips curved into smiles. Only one person broke out in song that way as he drove over the ridge on Watson's Hill, the summit on Roscoe Blvd. before the road dipped down into Sunland. Once again the beloved Parson and Aunt Jenny had returned home safely.

Parson Wornum made the community aware of his presence, and that of his wife Jenny, from the first day he arrived in Sunland circa 1902. Seven-year-old George Tench bounded down Sherman Grove Avenue en route to Rowley's general store in the early morning on an errand for his mother. An old man camped under an oak tree called to him to come meet his horses. Intrigued, George did as the man had asked. After acquainting George with the handsome pair of horses, the old man introduced himself as Parson Wornum and asked George to get permission from his mother to go for a ride with him. That morning they covered the entire community as the Parson invited each family for a 'meeting' the following Sunday.

At age 62, Parson Wornum had begun tending to the needs of a new congregation.

After serving in the 83rd Illinois Infantry during the Civil War, James Thomas Wornum,[2] one of the oldest of fourteen children in a family noted for its robustness and singing ability, followed in his father's footsteps and set out on his career as an itinerant preacher of the Free Methodist Church. Sometime during the 1890s, he met and married the younger Jenny Brocus Wornum.[3] Together they traveled across the country in a covered wooden wagon drawn by a team of sturdy horses.

From the back of his wagon, the Parson held services

From his wagon, the Parson held services
whenever he could gather enough worshippers.
Photo courtesy of Bolton Hall Museum.

whenever he could gather enough worshippers. A large man, standing tall on his makeshift pulpit, his booming voice ringing with confidence in himself and his religion, he could put "…the fear of God in man and beast."[4] Then while Jenny played a small piano, both erupted into song, usually one of their favorite hymns: "Christ Is Walking on the Water," "We'll Never Say Goodbye in Heaven," or "Lord, I'm Coming Home—Never More to Roam." Their clear, strong voices captivated many a listener.

Looking down Commerce Avenue, Tujunga, toward Foothill Blvd.
The post office (first building on the left) was located on the
southeast corner of Commerce and Valmont.
Photo courtesy of Bolton Hall Museum.

While the Parson and Aunt Jenny continued circuit-riding and preaching the gospel at camp meetings, they adopted Monte Vista Valley as their home base. No longer would the little white church in the park stand vacant. For many years, the couple walked arm in arm to Sunday services where the Parson proclaimed the Lord's word with the fervor and love that defined him. Aunt Jenny taught Sunday school, and the children fondly recall the piece of candy she gave each one of them as they parted at the door.

The Parson held Sunday services in the little church in Sunland Park. In 1942, the abandoned building was moved to Valaho and Thousand Oaks in Tujunga where it was enlarged and remodeled to become the Open Bible Church, then the Tujunga Foursquare Church.
Photo courtesy of Bolton Hall Museum.

But keeping souls healthy was not the only reason the Parson and Aunt Jenny became beloved and welcomed figures in the neighborhood. The Parson earned respect and quite a reputation as a horse trader. Two strong, well-groomed horses pulled his wagon or carried the familiar figures on their backs. He trained the animals himself so well, and without abuse, that they responded equally to a command or the touch of a child's hand.

Although the Parson dedicated his life to religion, he didn't expect the same of others. His tolerance and willingness to treat everyone equally endeared him to believers and skeptics alike. During the week, the Parson helped his neighbors in their gardens or lent a hand building a house or digging a cesspool. "…and never a family in the valley was in trouble, be it sickness, death or taxes, but the old man was on hand with a prayer or a strong arm and a willing back, or even a persuasive tongue, if somebody had to be talked out of something."[5]

The Parson Departs

Realizing his age and the approaching end, the Parson often entreated his friend Marshall V. Hartranft to donate land for a cemetery so he could be buried in the hills he loved so much. Hartranft, who owned and developed much of the land in early Tujunga, kept promising he would, but as happens with busy men, kept putting off any official action.

On April 10, 1922, Dr. Virginia T. Smith was called in to treat a very ill Parson. Days later, so ill that he could barely speak above a whisper, the Parson said to Hartranft, "I'm almost ready for it, Marsh, have you given my cemetery?"[6] Horrified, Hartranft dashed to his office and cancelled all appointments. It is certainly a tribute to the Parson that such a high profile entrepreneur would drop all business for the day to grant his friend's last wish.

Hartranft grabbed his maps and anxiously studied them. Finally, "He selected a site of about four acres of foothills, called in his superintendent of construction and told him to take all his laborers and all his mules and throw a road around the main hill. The next day he went to see the Parson. 'I have your cemetery now, Parson, it's all ready for you. You can check it out any time you want,' he told him. The old man smiled a contented smile and Mr. Hartranft added, 'but, I tell you something Parson, if you'll just stick around for a while we'll show you the swellest funeral you ever saw.' The Parson grinned and promised to do it."[7] He died the next morning at 11:30 a.m. in his home.

The entire community paid their respects to their beloved Parson, accompanying him on his final journey up Parson's Trail to the new Verdugo Hills Cemetery. Photo courtesy of Bolton Hall Museum.

And thus Parson Wornum became the first to be buried in Tujunga's Verdugo Hills Cemetery, also referred to as The Hills of Peace Cemetery, at the north end of

Pinyon Street in Tujunga. The Parson could not have asked for a more breathtaking spot, high in the hills, facing the setting sun, with a magnificent vista of the valley below.

His funeral reflected the community's love for their Parson. Thinking he would be uncomfortable in a fancy automobile, neighbors drove his body in his old wagon, pulled by his beloved horses, to the foot of the hill. From there they bore the coffin a quarter of a mile up the rough winding path, now called Parson's Trail, on their shoulders.

The Parson's old wagon and his faithful horses bore the Parson to the base of Parson's Trail. Photo courtesy of Bolton Hall Museum.

For three hours on that Saturday morning, mourners climbed, following their Parson to the summit and singing his favorite hymns. Even his old saddle horses, heads lowered almost to the ground, slowly clumped their way behind their master. Two buglers, one stationed at the grave and the other on a distant hilltop, sounded taps. Their playing reverberated across the valley just as the Parson's voice had once done.

Because of the Parson's service during the Civil War, he was accorded military honors by the American Legion.
Photo courtesy of Bolton Hall Museum.

John S. McGroarty, journalist for the *Los Angeles Times* who would later become a U.S. Congressman and the Poet Laureate of California, gave the Parson's eulogy. In days when religious denominations often clashed, no one thought it unusual for McGroarty, a devout Catholic, to lead the services for a Free Methodist. Respect for the Parson transcended such boundaries. His love had nourished the entire community and all called him friend.

McGroarty voiced his admiration. "…on the last Great Day … when he awakens, it shall be in no alien place, but in a spot well known of him and where he was well loved. His re-envisioned eyes shall behold again all with which he was so long familiar—the hills to which he lifted up his eyes and from which came his strength, the Mother Mountains at whose feet he prayed on bended knees and to whose high battlements he flung the challenge of his dauntless faith…"

Jenny died a year later and joined her husband on the highest knoll in the new cemetery. During the funeral service, John McGroarty envisioned the joy of them meeting again in another time and place. "I could see our strong old Parson … sitting on his horse, erect in the saddle as he used to sit when he rode about these hills and valleys … And beside him was another horse, waiting with an empty saddle … when the jasper gate swung open, the old Parson reached down and helped Aunt Jenny up to the waiting saddle and they galloped away…"[9]

Familiar figures on horseback ride down
Michigan Avenue (Foothill Blvd.)
Photo Courtesy of Bolton Hall Museum.

His Cemetery

Respect for the Parson and his burial place waned over the years. Drinking parties layered the cemetery with beer cans that rusted with age. Vandals pushed over gravestones, pulled off bronze and wooden markers, and even broke into the mausoleum, built in later years, to pull out bodies and scatter ashes. Weeds thrived, choking pathways and obscuring markers.

By the 1970s, the abhorrent conditions of the cemetery prompted numerous complaints. The State Cemetery Board of Directors met in February of 1971 with owners Reverend Kenton Beshore and his wife Lois Anderson about draining and erosion problems. Although the Beshores assured the Board that preliminary work had already begun for correcting the problems, by April the Beshores had to be issued an Order to Comply by the Department of Building and Safety of the City of Los Angeles to insist that they fix the grading problems.

For the next several years, newspaper headlines screamed about the plight of the cemetery, and about the

District Attorney's and State Cemetery Board's probes into the problems there. Questions arose about the misuse of endowment funds and false statements in contracts with clients. Poorly-kept records prevented clear identification of burial sites. The stench of decay seeped from unsealed mausoleum vaults. Inspections of the cemetery revealed 130 unplaced headstones and cremated remains of seven people dumped on a trash pile behind an A-frame work shed. And what did all the 'sound and fury' accomplish? The grading and erosion problems remained—sure ingredients for a catastrophe in an area with a history of periodic heavy floods.

Heavy rains tore open graves and sent corpses tumbling down the hillside.
Photo from The Record-Ledger, February 16, 1978.

And sure enough, nature supplied the final assault when heavy rains soaked the land in 1978. A little after midnight on February 9th, thunderous reverberations awoke neighbors. Some said it sounded like an earthquake; others like a train racing down Parson's Trail. A large chunk of the ground broke loose, creating a landslide that sent rocks and debris crashing down the hillside. The force of the tumbling wreckage tore open graves. In the morning, horrified homeowners found 30 bodies strewn among the refuse in their yards.[10]

A Tujunga resident stares at the leg of a corpse that washed down into her yard. Photo from the Glendale NewsPress, February 10, 1978.

City taxpayers paid a hefty $50,000 bill for emergency work after the flood. Now a public health hazard, the cemetery could no longer be ignored. Obviously, the bodies that washed down the hillside had to be re-casketed and re-interred. But the slide also exposed other graves through which lizards and other rodents darted about. Workers exhumed additional bodies to relocate them on safer ground.[11] Debris that included pieces of concrete liners and rotting wood caskets had to be cleared from roads and the hillside. And still the erosion problem needed to be solved.

In May 1980, the Beshores resigned as managers, but apparently their Institute of Christian Research remained owners.[12] The Beshores transferred reins to caretaker Bonnie Mason, who disappeared a year or so later. Without anyone on the premises, the City of Los Angeles stepped in several times in the early 1980s to clear hazardous brush and threatened to file a lawsuit against the Beshores at the Institute for unpaid bills.

Finally in December 1984, the court granted the State Cemetery Board conservatorship of the cemetery and management of the endowment funds. Unfortunately, the change did not make a big difference. In 1994, state cemetery officials voted to evict Frank Gatti, caretaker since 1988. Gatti's use of the run-down commercial A-frame 'work shed' as a home for his wife and seven children violated City codes. He also failed to pay the utility bills. After that, the water supply was shut off.

Years of neglect and human indifference have destroyed the final resting place of more than 3,000 people. As of 1999, little was being done to restore the cemetery or to provide basic maintenance. Thanks to the diligence of The Friends of the Hills of Peace Cemetery, some records now exist as to who is buried in the cemetery, but not always where. The removal of grave markers, the erosion and shifting of the earth, the mass reburials, and the negligence of caretakers have made it impossible to identify many individual gravesites.

Residents clean up the grisly devastation on the corner of Parson's Trail and Pinyon Street. Photo from The Record-Ledger, March 6, 1978.

And what about the beloved Parson? "The Parson's grave remained secure atop his rocky knoll, safe and sound on 'Higher Ground'."[13] In one sense, this is true. The first burial sites atop a small hill were not affected by the landslides, and thus, the graves remain undisturbed by the rains. But the exact location of the Parson is unknown. Vandals removed or destroyed the monument marking his grave. The Parson's original wood grave marker, rescued from destruction in the past, now reposes in Bolton Hall Museum.

#####

Route to the Verdugo Hills Cemetery

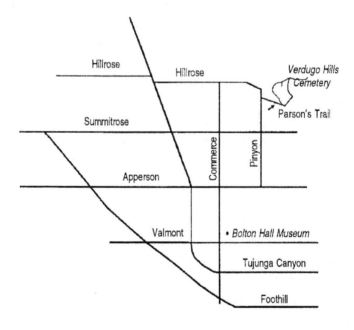

Footnotes

[1] The natural acoustics in the valley allowed sound to carry for miles. Buildings later absorbed much of the sound.

[2] James Thomas Wornum: born August 1, 1839 – died April 19, 1922.

[3] Jenny Brocus Wornum: born 1855 – died November 15, 1923. Sources show three different spellings of Jenny's maiden name: Brocos, Brocus, Brocous. Brocus if used in this document because it is the spelling used in correspondence sent by a relative to Bolton Hall Museum.

[4] Carson, Viola L., "Lord, I'm Coming Home—Never More to Roam," March 31, 1978, p. 2.

[5] Hatch, Mabel, "Horsetrading Parson Finally Got Cemetery," *The Record-Ledger, Historical & Progress Edition*, May 21, 1953, Section B, p. 5.

[6] Ibid., p. 5.

[7] Ibid., p. 5.

[8] "Parson Laid to Rest in Hills," *The Los Angeles Times*, April 24, 1922, Part II.

[9] "Pioneers Go to Their Reward," *The Record-Ledger*, Thursday, November 1, 1923.

[10] "Corpses Among Debris," *The Record-Ledger*, Saturday, March 11, 1978.

[11] Accounts differ on the actual number of bodies that needed to be relocated. One newspaper account claims 42; cemetery records indicate the number may be higher.

[12] Some documents list the Institute of Christian Research as owners, others the Hills of Peace (Cemetery). The City of Los Angeles letter threatening the lawsuit is addressed to both. Apparently the Hills of

Peace is a DBA (Doing Business As) for the Institute.

[13] Carlson, Viola L. "Lord, I'm Coming Home—Never More to Roam," March 31, 1978, p. 6.

Bibliography

"Administer Suspends V.H. Cemetery Burials." *The Record-Ledger*, September 24, 1975.

"Bodies of Pioneers Rest on Hilltop." Clippings file, Bolton Hall Museum.

Bogert, John M. "Legislators Look at Cemeteries." *Glendale NewsPress*, August 14, 1976.

Carlson Viola L. "Lord, I'm Coming Home—Never More to Roam." (Essay) March 31, 1978.

Cemetery Board, State of California. Correspondence from the files of The Friends of the Hills of Peace Cemetery.

"Cemetery Directors Fix Prices." *The Record-Ledger*, February 8, 1923.

"Church Transformation." *The Record-Ledger*, Thursday, May 21, 1953.

City of Los Angeles, California. Correspondence from the files of The Friends of the Hills of Peace Cemetery.

Colville, Lucy. "Verdugo Hills Cemetery—No Peace for the Dead." *The Record-Ledger*, Thursday, April 12, 1973.

"Corpses Await Reburial." *The Record-Ledger*, Thursday, February 16, 1978.

"Corpses Among Debris." *The Record-Ledger*, February 11, 1978.

Crowell, T. Michael. "Grisly Aftermath of Flood: Cemetery Bodies Unearthed." *Glendale NewsPress*, Saturday, February 11, 1978.

Department of Building and Safety, City of Los Angeles. Correspondence from the files of The Friends of the Hills of Peace Cemetery.

"Directors Inspect Cemetery Ground." *The Record-Ledger*, January 28, 1923.

"Directors Tackle Cemetery Plans." *The Record-Ledger*, January 11, 1923.

"Foothill Flood Evacuation." *Glendale NewsPress*, Friday, February 10, 1978.

Freidman, Robert A. "Old Parson's Cemetery Is Given New Life." *The Star (Glendale NewsPress)*. September 4, 1968.

Hatch, Mabel. "Hills of Peace Restoration Is Urged by Mabel Hatch." *The Record-Ledger*, Thursday, June 9, 1955.

Hatch, Mabel. "Horsetrading Parson Finally Got Cemetery." *The Record-Ledger, Historical & Progress Edition*, May 21, 1953, Section B, p. 5.

Herrera, Arlene. Report of the Verdugo Hills Cemetery. 1955.

Hitt, Marlene. "Beloved Sunland Preacher Given a Memorable Send-off." *The Leader*, March 21, 1998.

James T. Wornum. California State Board of Health: Standard Certificate of Death. April 24, 1922.

Little Landers Historical Society. Docent Handbook. Bolton Hall Museum.

Lubas, Ken. "Deluge Sweeps 30 Bodies from Graves into Yards." *The Los Angeles Times*, Saturday, February 11, 1978.

Martinez, Al. "3 Die, 10 Sought, 30 Bodies Washed from Cemetery." *The Los Angeles Times*, Friday, February 10, 1978.

McKee, Bob. "Cemetery Probe Seeks Endowment Accounting." *The Ledger*, Thursday, August 26, 1976.

McKee, Bob. "Tujunga Cemetery Condition Probed." *The Ledger*, Thursday, August 11, 1976.

Nichols, Roberta. "6 Proposals Drawn to Aid Verdugo Hills Cemetery." *The Los Angeles Times*, Sunday, February 19, 1984.

Noguchi, Thomas T. *Coroner*. New York, NY: Simon & Schuster. 1983.

"Old Parson Packed Church in Wagon to Bring Religion to Little Landers." Clippings file, Bolton Hall Museum.

Olson, Jennifer. "Accusations Surface in Verdugo Cemetery Affairs." *The Record-Ledger,* March 24, 1977.

Parcher, Carroll. "Snow Sports More Like Self Torture." *The Leader,* Wednesday, February 22, 1984.

"Parson Laid to Rest in Hills." Clippings file, Bolton Hall Museum.

"Parson Laid to Rest in Hills." *The Los Angeles Times*, April 24, 1922. Part II.

"Parson of the Green Verdugo Hills." Clippings file. Bolton Hall Museum.

"Parson Told on Deathbed that Cemetery Was Ready for Him." *The Record-Ledger*, May 21, 1953.

"Parson's Family Visits Cemetery." *The Record-Ledger*, Monday, March 6, 1978.

"Pick Out Your Lot in the Tujunga Cemetery Friday." *The Record-Ledger*, Thursday, December 4, 1924.

"Pioneers Go to Their Reward." *The Record-Ledger*, Thursday, November 1, 1923.

"Plan Improvements at Hills of Peace." *The Record-Ledger*, July 23, 1959.

Pottage, Mike. "DA Investigators Probe Verdugo Hills Cemetery." *The Ledger*, Thursday, August 21, 1976.

Quinn, James, "Criminal Action May Be Filed in Cemetery Case." *The Los Angeles Times*, April 13, 1977.

Records of the Hills of Peace Cemetery: Compiled June 1993. Bolton Hall Museum.

"Reincarnation of Church." *The Record-Ledger*, Thursday, May 21, 1953.

Schell, A. Elizabeth. Letter to Mary Lou Pozzo. August 1996.

Schubert, Mary. "Cemetery Officials to Evict Caretaker." *Daily News*, August 2, 1994.

Schubert, Mary. "State Checking on Tujunga Cemetery." *Daily News*, July 2, 1994.

Shaffer, Gina. "Vandals, Floods Disturb Hillside Cemetery's Rest." *Daily News*, Sunday, April 19, 1987.

"Start Cemetery As Resting Place for Pioneers." *The Record-Ledger*, 1938.

Tench, George. Personal interview by Viola Carlson. April 15, 1983.

"Tujunga Cemetery Ass'n Needs Development Funds." *The Record-Ledger*, Thursday, July 26, 1956.

"Uneasy Peace." *The Los Angeles Times*, July 27, 1978.

From Crackers to Coal Oil

**"We were used to taking life
as we found it."**

The Early History of Sunland, California
Volume 4

ML Tiernan

When a student pulled out his gun and laid it on his desk, the tiny one-room school found itself needing a new teacher. That brought Virginia Newcomb, a romance, and a new family that helped to develop the town, leaving behind a detailed account of pioneer life in a small village.

From Crackers to Coal Oil

A gun in the schoolroom leads to romance and marriage.

**The Early History of Sunland, California
Volume 4**

ML Tiernan

From Crackers to Coal Oil

www.maryleetiernan.com
Second printing April 1, 2015
10 9 8 7 6 5 4 3 2

ISBN 978-0983067238 (Paperback)

Photograph on cover courtesy of Bolton Hall Museum, Tujunga, California.
Quote on cover is from an interview with the Rowleys.

Contents

Trouble in the Schoolroom

A mid-year crisis in the schoolroom! It was not the usual problem of rain swelling the Big Tujunga River, thus making the road across the wash impassible. With so few families in Sunland, the children attended the original school built in 1888 in Little Tujunga, or Tujunga Terrace[1],

The original schoolhouse in Little Tujunga, or Tujunga Terrace, later named Lake View Terrace. Photo courtesy of Bolton Hall Museum.

later renamed Lake View Terrace.

Any heavy rain prevented travel on the dirt roads in Sunland, which were really little more than narrow passages with two ruts worn from wagon wheels. The road across the wash completely flooded, ensuring the children a day off from school.

This time the crisis came from within the school itself. Pioneer children led the same rugged life as their parents who were carving a living out of harsh land. They often walked miles to and from school. The boys sometimes carried guns to shoot jackrabbits for sport, or to kill deadly snakes for safety. The young schoolmaster, apparently not used to the boys' rough ways and wanting to establish stricter discipline, cut willow switches and brought them to school. He laid them on his desk as a warning against their antics. In turn, one of the boys pulled out his knife and another his gun, and imitating the teacher, placed the weapons on their desks.

On the way home from school that day, the teacher heard shots and felt the wind from the bullets as they whistled by his ears. Although a contemporary claimed it was just "the boys having good clean fun,"[2] the schoolmaster quit. Without a teacher, the bell no longer rang in the morning to summon the children to the one-room schoolhouse.

A New Teacher

By 1891, Loron Thomas Rowley[3] played a central role in anything that happened in the village of Sunland. He immediately wrote to his brother Quintin, a doctor living in Downey, inquiring about a candidate to replace the schoolmaster. In reply, Quintin sent twenty-one-year-old Virginia Florence Newcomb, graduate of the Normal School in Los Angeles.[4]

Born the same year her parents arrived from Mississippi to help establish the town of Downey, Virginia knew the difficulties of pioneer life in a struggling village. She walked into the same situation as her predecessor, but better prepared. As a younger child in a large family of boys, years of dealing with her brothers would help her handle Sunland's youth. Her father, a sergeant who fought during the Civil War under General Robert E. Lee, also advised her on how to deal with the 'upstarts.' With Virginia, order returned to the schoolroom.

Loron helped Virginia settle in—and more. While she taught for the next two years, he also courted her. The ten years' difference in their ages mattered little to either of them. When they married in 1893, he brought her to his homestead in an area in Tujunga later named Seven Hills.

Springs from the mountain provided her new home in Rowley Canyon with plenty of water for home, garden, and crops, at least for most of the year. Only in late summer did the flow of water cease. The blessings of plentiful water outweighed the problems of living in the canyon—the boulders that crashed down during the rain or the coyotes that howled through the night from their dens in the wash.

The first one-room schoolhouse in Sunland located in Sunland Park. Photo courtesy of Mrs. Elizabeth Schell.

Loron Rowley

For both Loron and Virginia, the greatest drawback to pioneer life was not having enough time to read. Like his wife, Loron was well-educated. He loved to quote from Homer's *Iliad* and recite the works of his favorite poet, Robert Burns, imitating Burns' Scottish dialect. Loren's education had come to an abrupt end during his senior year at the University of Minnesota.

The depression in the Midwest after the Civil War forced many farmers to abandon their land and migrate. Loron's family also sought to escape starving conditions. Colorful brochures and posters published by the railroads promised a high yield of land for farming in the glorious climate of California. That, combined with the low rail-rates, prompted Loron to leave Minnesota and scout for government land where the family could re-establish itself.

Loron joined the flow of migrants and boarded the Southern Pacific for points west.[5] During his first year in California, Loron joined two uncles who lived in Mandeville Canyon, raising bees and selling honey. While learning the in's and out's of this profitable business, he kept his ears open for news about government land available for homesteading. In 1882, he found such land in the Monte Vista Valley. So he loaded some hives into a buckboard, drove up through Glendale, pitched a tent, and homesteaded 160 acres. With the help of the Verdugo family[6], he built a ranch house.

Despite its 'failure' during the land boom, the village of farmers continued to grow. Photo courtesy of Bolton Hall Museum.

Besides establishing his beehives and raising cattle, Loron marketed the wood he chopped on the ranch by carting it out of the canyon on sleds and transporting it by wagon into Los Angeles. Few people lived in the valley at that time, before the impending Land Boom, because the poor roads—or lack of them—discouraged settlement. For the woodcutters, however, Monte Vista Valley furnished a lucrative business. Los Angles needed wood as fuel for cooking and heating. The abundant supply of native greasewood and pine trees that grew along the fringes of the mountains and in the canyons quite literally went up in smoke in L.A. By the 1890s, the denuded forests would need replanting.

While Loron struggled to raise cattle and keep the beehives productive, the developers arrived. At first, he hired on as a construction worker, but seeing the need for supplies for the workers, he contracted with the promoters in 1885 to build a two-story structure on the southwest corner of Central Avenue and First Street (later Fenwick and Oro Vista) for mail distribution and a general store which sold everything from crackers to coal oil. Loron would go by wagon to L.A. to buy supplies, stay overnight, and come back the next day.

Most of the mail, which Loron picked up at the Roscoe train station, came for workmen building the Monte Vista Hotel. When the Land Boom collapsed in 1888, many of the original land purchasers disappeared, as did much of Loron's business. During this period, Virginia arrived to teach school. After they married, Virginia shared the growing pains of Loron's enterprises while they continued to develop the ranch and began raising a family with the birth of their son Eustace in 1896.

Although Loron was ill-suited for rough work because

a bout with typhoid fever in his youth left him with troublesome legs, the needs of his family outweighed his own personal problems. When he'd established himself in the valley, he sent for the family. His father Asa joined him around 1888 and homesteaded land adjacent to Loron's. His sister Mary Grace followed shortly thereafter and staked her land south of theirs. Loron and his father continued with the productive bees, but changed from cattle to planting olive groves, peach orchards, and alfalfa. The three Rowley homesteads covered much of the land from Big Tujunga Canyon along the base of the mountain towards La Crescenta. With land they bought or quitclaimed in the ensuing years, the family ended up owning over 1,000 acres.

The Rowley Family

When the promoter Frank H. Barclay lost his land in the demise of the Land Boom, he also lost the Monte Vista Hotel. The hotel remained vacant into the 1890s, when Loron's brother Quintin bought it as an investment. He persuaded Loron and Virginia to move into the hotel to guard his investment. Here their second son Robert (1898)

Robert and Eustace Rowley (back) with their Aunt Marion. Most roads In Sunland were little more than narrow passages with two ruts worn from wagon wheels. Photo courtesy of Bolton Hall Museum.

and their first daughter Dorothy (1902) were born. Virginia had her hands full with the adventurous Robert. He liked to climb on the balconies, chase bats out from the belfry, and race his bike around the porch that encircled the hotel. Once he climbed up on the roof to slide down, nearly killing himself.

Lack of medical care in the valley made accidents or illness a very serious threat. Midwives delivered children, or at least attended to the mother until a doctor could arrive. Many births were never recorded. Imagine the irony these children experienced later in life having to prove they existed before they could get a birth certificate.

A family often had to seek medical assistance outside the valley. When Dorothy Rowley fell off Jenny Wornum's horse and broke her arm, her parents had to race four and a half miles through the rain to the train depot and then wait to flag down the next train to reach Burbank where a doctor could set her arm. How agonizing must those hours have been for both the injured Dorothy and her anxious parents. Before modern medicines, such as antibiotics, even a doctor could not ensure a cure for ailments that today may seem commonplace. The youngest Rowley, Clara Virginia, would die at age 14 from an ear infection.

Often pioneers either suffered through an ailment or depended on home remedies. Virginia insisted on serving her 'Senna tea' as a prescription for every affliction, be it a headache or a stomach ache. When a neighbor fell sick, Virginia could be counted on to appear with some of her tea. She served it both internally as a purge, or externally, as a poultice soaked in tea water with turpentine as the equivalent of an antibiotic.

Ranchers did continue to buy large acreage in the valley during the 1880s and 1890s. They planted orchards, vineyards, and olive groves on the lower side of the valley, where water was available. The ever-industrious Loron began hauling this produce from the valley—grapes, oranges, lemons—first in his wagon, then by truck, and established the first freight line in the valley. Some of the ranch owners did not live on the land themselves, but hired

Wentworth Ave. looking toward Sherman Grove Ave.
The slope of the road caused flooding during rains.
Photo courtesy of Bolton Hall Museum.

others to work it. This brought in additional families who supported the store and post office and the eventual opening of Sunland's own school.

By 1900 Loron operated the store and the ranch and his hauling business, but another down-market made money tight. A job opened in the newly formed government Forest Service, which reforested mountains that had burned or been denuded by the woodcutters. So Loron became Sunland's first forest ranger. With all his enterprises, Loron needed help. Virginia stepped in and became the first postmistress of Sunland, a position she kept until 1908. When Mrs. Huse replaced Virginia as postmistress, she, too, worked another job—as correspondent for the Glendale newspaper. She wrote a column once a week about news she gleaned by reading the postcards that came and went in the mail.

The children, too, did their part to help. When Loron began hauling produce by truck from the valley to Los Angeles, the uncooperative Cadillac often broke down. Since he couldn't repair it himself, he hitched a horse to it to pull it all the way to a garage in Burbank. Intrigued by the engine, as boys often are, Robert began tinkering with it until he learned to fix it, saving his father both time and money. Sometimes, however, Robert and the other village boys used their knowledge of cars a bit deviously. Breakdowns being common, when Dr. Speighs's car refused to start after church, he thought little of giving the boys 50 cents to start it for him. What would he have thought if he knew that while he was in church, the boys disconnected a part, and then simply reconnected it, to earn their 50 cents?

Virginia insisted on education for her children, rudimentary as it might be in a one-room school, where lessons focused on 'the three R's,' geography, and spelling. Missing school every time the river swelled from rain and wiped out the road interfered with those lessons.

Community picnic in Sunland Park. The park was the center of community social activities: picnics, sports, and holiday festivities, including a parade on July 4th.
Photo courtesy of Bolton Hall Museum.

The children may not have minded, but Virginia did. To circumvent the problem, the Rowleys helped start a new school, right in the center of town—in the park.[7] The new Sunland School, however, soon ran into another problem. To qualify for county money, six children needed to attend the school. One year, attendance fell to five. Not to be defeated by such regulations, Virginia enrolled her second son, Robert, at age four and a half, as the sixth child.

When Quintin Rowley sold the Monte Vista Hotel in 1903, the family moved back to the ranch house in Seven Hills. From there, the boys walked two miles to school. To amuse themselves on the way, they sometimes brought along the family's 12-guage Winchester pump gun to shoot rabbits for target practice. After the incident that had originally brought Virginia to Sunland, the policy about guns in school—and discipline in general—had changed. The boys hid the gun before entering school so the teacher wouldn't take it away from them. Their teacher kept a firm hand on his students. If they misbehaved, he'd crack their fingers. But sometimes students enjoy a little payback. Once, when the class went to the pasture to collect mistletoe, the teacher got caught in a bog. The kids heard his cries, but just let him stew for a while before coming to his rescue.

Living in an area known for its hunting of deer, dove, and quail, it was not unusual for local boys to develop an avid interest in the sport. When son Robert insisted at too early an age to go hunting with his uncles, Virginia's experience with handling boys served her well. Concerned with his safety, yet not wanting to crush his spirits, Virginia allowed her son to discover the truth for himself. She placed a shotgun in his hands. When Robert fired, the recoil knocked him over backwards. The day he could fire the gun without being knocked over, Virginia allowed Robert to join the hunting parties.

The new, enlarged Sunland School when it moved
from Sunland Park to Hillrose Street.
Photo courtesy of Marshall Murray.

Shooting was more than a sport for early settlers. Even the women and kids learned to shoot for protection. Whether trudging through miles of sagebrush and cactus on a hike or horseback ride, or on the way to swimming holes in the Big Tujunga wash, they often ran into rattlesnakes along the way. And the canyons still teemed with wildlife. Although Virginia cooped her chickens to protect them, the coyotes still managed to steal into the hen house at night. In years to come, her boys would jump out of bed and grab their guns during the ruckus of a raid, with hopes of killing a coyote as they chased them off.

Hunting put meat on the table. Individuals shot jackrabbits and quail for family dinners, but when someone shot big game, the whole town came to carve it up and share the spoils. The first time thirteen-year-old Robert shot a deer, he proudly tried to imitate the men and lift it onto his shoulders, but failed. The deer weighed five pounds more than he did. The Rowley brothers often brought deer back from their hunting trips to the canyon and shared the meat with neighbors. To keep meat from spoiling, Virginia covered it with gunny sacks, kept wet with water, to keep it cool.

Back to Town

With business centered in town and the boys in school, living out on the ranch proved difficult at times. So in 1905, the Rowleys built the first rock house in Sunland on Hill Street near Flower Avenue (later Hillrose and Floralita). The backyard accommodated Virginia's flock of chickens and her vegetable garden. In the pasture next to

Sunland store circa 1913, believed to the Rowleys'.
Photo courtesy of Bolton Hall Museum.

the house, where running water from a spring kept grass growing all year on the damp ground, the family kept horses and milking cows. Virginia taught each of her children to milk the cows as soon as they were old enough to carry a bucket. As they grew, they were also expected to help in the store.

Once Marion forgot she was supposed to be tending the store and went off with her friends instead. A customer came, needing a pan. Finding no one to wait on her, she helped herself and left a note explaining what she had done: "I left 25 cents. Thought that about right. If not, let me know."[8] Luckily for Marion, stealing, either the merchandise or the money in the cash register, did not fit the pioneer character. They all worked too hard and respected one another's efforts.

The kitchen stove and two fireplaces in the new home kept the downstairs well-heated during cold weather. But upstairs, the bedrooms remained cold. At night, the children went to bed with a rock, inscribed with their name, which had been warmed in the fireplace. They wrapped the rock in old newspaper and put it in the bed to keep their feet warm. Since Smuggle, their cat, did not have a personal rock, she just crawled right into the fireplace to keep warm—and usually walked around with slightly singed fur.

Virginia counted on Sunday to bring the family

together after a hectic week. After services at the Free Methodist Church, she picked a hen no longer laying eggs, and the boys killed it for their traditional chicken-and-dumplings family dinner. She gathered beans, carrots, and other vegetables from her garden and made biscuits and cornbread. Their peach orchards provided fruit, fresh or preserved, depending on the season. After a hearty mid-day meal, Sunday night light supper consisted of a mixture of honey and butter poured over hot biscuits and more peaches. Virginia's daughter Dorothy later regretted never being able to duplicate dumplings as delectable as those her mother made.

The Rowleys built one of the first rock houses in Sunland, on Hillrose near Floralita. Photo courtesy of Bolton Hall Museum.

Claims about Sunland's clean, healthy air must have had some validity. In spite of Virginia's hectic schedule keeping two homes—the ranch and the newer house on Hillrose—cooking, raising chickens, and growing vegetables, and her job as postmistress and mother of five, and her husband's enterprises with the general store, forestry service, orchards, and newer delivery service of groceries, newspapers, and milk to farms and families in the now developing town of Tujunga, the family still found time to gather in the evenings on the front porch, where the children played jacks or practiced their musical instruments.

The Rowley house in 1999.

Each member of the family showed musical ability, and Virginia insisted the children take music lessons from Walter Maygrove, the local music virtuoso. Although music primarily served as family entertainment, when Bolton Hall opened in Tujunga, Virginia, Loron, and Eustace played for the Saturday night dances: folk and square dances or Virginia reels for the older generation; waltzes and the two-step for the younger.

Regardless of how much the family liked living in town and being together, they could not entirely vacate the ranch. Families continued to move into the valley. Some bought land; some quitclaimed deeds. A person could quitclaim land by occupying it and paying taxes for over five years, then go to court and claim it, even though someone else might hold papers. The paper holder had to pay taxes, work on the land or live on it, to retain ownership. Many of the people who had bought land from Barclay during the Land Boom did not occupy the land. Worse, they had been given unrecorded deeds from an unrecorded lithograph map, which didn't have much value in court. Some parcels of the same land had been sold several times. It took 20 years of lawsuits to straighten out who owned what.

The Rowleys themselves took advantage of the quitclaim process and acquired more land in town. But they also feared that someone might try to quitclaim their homestead. Virginia often stayed at the ranch with her youngest daughters, Marion (born 1906) and Clara Virginia (born 1908). Without other means available, the family invented their own system of communication. At a prearranged hour, Virginia waved a lantern to signal the family below that she and the girls were okay.

When Eustace and Robert finished elementary school, they went to Burbank High School. They hitched a ride with the buggy on the mail run to Roscoe Station at 5:50, caught the train at 6:00, and arrived in Burbank before school opened. On the way home, however, they walked the five miles uphill to get home. For Robert's second year, the boys switched to the smaller, but closer, San Fernando High. Their father gave them a horse and buggy to drive the 10 miles to school; a barn in the yard provided shelter for the horse during the day. Robert's graduating class in 1915 consisted of 17 students. Although the boys managed the difficult trek to school, Virginia felt the route too demanding for her daughters.

In 1918, the family moved to Glendale so Dorothy, Marion, and Clara Virginia could attend Glendale High School. Two years later, Virginia's cousin William Nance bought the general store, and Loron became a truant officer for the Glendale School District. The family sold off their land. In 1922, James T. Fitzgerald bought the 160-acre homestead in Seven Hills for $24,000. During the Great

Depression, Robert sold some of the acreage in town; after World War II, he sold what remained.

The Rowley family may be gone from Sunland, but they have left traces of their presence. Their namesakes—Rowley Canyon and Rowley Place in Seven Hills—bear witness to these early settlers. Their house at 8436 Hillrose is occupied by another family who, fortunately, has preserved one of Sunland's earliest landmarks.

#####

Footnotes

[1] When the colony of Little Lands decided to rename itself and call the town Tujunga, it caused confusion because Little Tujunga—later Lake View Terrace—already existed. Old timers were both amused and annoyed by the repetition of the name.

[2] Rowley, Robert. *Sunland-Tujunga.*

[3] Loron Thomas Rowley: born June 3, 1860 – died May 31, 1942.

[4] Virginia Florence Newcomb Rowley: born 1870 – died March 1938. A Normal School was an institute for training teachers.

[5] For a description of traveling accommodations on the trains and the railroad price-fare wars, see *Volume 1, Hotels of the Hopeful.*

[6] The Verdugo family's Mexican land grant included parts of Glendale, La Crescenta, and La Canada.

[7] The school was probably located in the northeast corner of Sunland Park.

[8] Personal interview with Marion Rowley by Charles Miller.

Bibliography

"Blumfields Have Resided in Same House on Sherman Grove Since 1906 Marriage." *The Record-Ledger*, September 30, 1954.

"Born at Old Monte Vista Hotel, Speaker Revives Past of Area." *The Record-Ledger*, February 11, 1971.

Colville, Lucy. "Rowley Recalls Early Days of Sunland-Tujunga." *The Record-Ledger*, September, 1973.

"First School in the Sunland Tujunga Valley." *The Record-Ledger*, Historical & Progress Edition, May 21, 1953.

"First Sunland School Founded about 1898 in 1-Room Building." *The Record-Ledger*, Historical & Progress Edition, May 21, 1953.

Lombard, Sarah. "Monte Vista = Sunland." *The Record-Ledger*, September 22, 1977.

Lombard, Sarah. "Verdant Valley Attracts Settlers." *The Record-Ledger*, October 13, 1977.

"Public School, Monte Vista." *The Record-Ledger*, Historical & Progress Edition, May 21, 1953.

Rowley, Dorothy. Personal interview by Joan Conrad, Viola Carlson, and Mary Lou Pozzo. February 17, 1996.

Rowley, Marion. Personal interview by Charles Miller. June 27, 1986.

Rowley, Robert. Personal interview by Viola Carlson. 1974.

Rowley, Robert. *Sunland-Tujunga.*

"Sunland School Nears 70 Years at Same Site." *The Record-Ledger*, July 3, 1975.

Sunland-Tujunga: Nestled between the Verdugo Hills and the San Gabriel Mts. The Sunland-Tujunga Chamber of Commerce, March, 1947.

He Never Came Home

The Mysterious Disappearance that Devastated a Family

**"He had made many enemies, and
many there were who would like revenge."**

The Early History of Sunland, California
Volume 5

ML Tiernan

Joe Ardizzone, a local grape-grower, doubled as a hit-man for the Mafia. During Prohibition, Joe's bootlegging activities caught him in the middle of in-house quarreling. In 1931, he left on a short trip and disappeared into the pages of history.

He Never Came Home

Joe Ardizzone climbs into his car and drives into the pages of history.

**The Early History of Sunland, California
Volume 5**

ML Tiernan

He Never Came Home

www.maryleetiernan.com
Second printing April 1, 2015
10 9 8 7 6 5 4 3 2

ISBN 978-0983067245 (Paperback)

Photograph on cover courtesy of the Ardizone family. Quote on cover from *The Grim Reapers*, p. 165.

Contents

Elsie

When Elsie Elizabeth Ellenberg arrived in California with her family in 1912, Sunland was already a small country town. The post office and telephone company connected the community to the world. Children attended school. The Free Methodist and Sunland Baptist churches

Pioneer women often carried rifles for protection against wildlife, especially snakes. Elsie (left) and her sister Frances (right) pose in the open vistas characteristic of early Sunland. Photo courtesy of the Ardizone family.

offered Sunday services. Families gathered for picnics, concerts, parades, and other social activities in the park. Automobiles transported passengers to Glendale in the east and to the train or to San Fernando in the west. Two hotels, the elegant Monte Vista and the smaller Park, offered amenities to travelers and vacationing families.

Although residents may have been proud of the progress of their flourishing community, Elsie may have felt she had taken a step back in time. The automobiles bumped over pitted, dirt roads. The telephone worked only a few hours a day. A private home housed the post office. Grizzly bears still roamed through wooded canyons. Open vistas of mountains and acres of citrus and olive trees greeted her instead of the crowded, busy streets of the world she left behind.

Born in 1898, Elsie spent her childhood in New York City. When Elsie was nine, her mother died. Her father moved the children—Elsie and her younger brother and sister, John and Frances—to the home of their grandparents John and Margaret Ellenberg, German immigrants who lived on the second story above their general store. Her father, also named John, continued working as a jewelry engraver, but kept reading about the golden opportunities in California. Elsie's grandparents threatened never to speak to him again if he took the children out West, but the lure of opportunity outweighed the threat. Despite their protests, John packed up his children and boarded a train for the land of sunshine.

So at age 14, Elsie found herself living in a lean-to while her father built a ranch house for $600. The family erected their temporary shelter some distance from town along a dirt road surrounded by fields of sagebrush.[1] Since her father's job in downtown Los Angeles meant a very long commute in those days, care of her brother and sister, including cooking their meals outside on an open fire, fell to Elsie. For pleasure, she enjoyed horseback riding and hiking the local mountain trails, although she quickly learned to carry a gun as protection against coyotes, snakes, bobcats, and other wildlife.

A year later, Elsie met a neighbor riding on horseback through the fields near her home. The six-foot, 25-year-old Joe (Joseph) Ardizzone[2] obviously made an impression. The handsome Italian spoke little English, and Elsie spoke no Italian, but romance has its own language. They married a year afterward, in 1916.

Elsie Ardizzone in newly planted vineyards.
Photo courtesy of Mrs. Josephine Kemp.

The Ardizzones

The Ardizzones came from Sicily, home of the Mafia. Legend credits the beginning of the Mafia to an incident that occurred in the city of Palermo, on March 30, 1282, while the French governed Sicily. A drunken French sergeant, Pierre Druet, accosted a bride-to-be on her way to the church. Terrified, the girl tore away from the Frenchman, fell, and cracked her skull on the church wall. The grief-stricken bridegroom beat the sergeant, screaming "Morte alla Francia!" ("Death to all the French!")

Other Sicilians picked up his cry as the news spread and changed it slightly to "Morte alla Francia Italia anela!" ("Death to the French is Italy's cry!") In the ensuing uprising, most of the French in Sicily were killed. A secret society formed, aimed at protecting poor or ill-treated Sicilians. The society shortened the cry to M-A-F-I-A for its name.[3]

Even though the Ardizzones already owned property in Los Angeles, they bought land in Sunland in the early 1900s. The terrain and weather closely resembled that of their native Sicily, a suitable place for growing grapes from the cuttings brought from Italy. Their vineyards, just to the north of the Ellenberg property, included a house, although they usually stayed there only during the grape harvest.

When Joe and Elsie married, Elsie's father gave them his house and moved to Los Angles with his two younger children. Through the years, Joe transformed the barren fields surrounding it. Most of the acreage, of course, nourished grapevines. Around the house, he first added driveways and fences; then he planted. Truck after truck from the Armstrong nursery arrived with trees, shrubbery, and flowers.

The Ellenberg home later became the Ardizzone residence. On the left is the lean-to where the family lived while building the house. The site became the location of Mt. Gleason Jr. High School. Photo courtesy of Mrs. J. Kemp.

Lawn replaced sagebrush. The trees blossomed and produced plums, apricots, peaches, figs, pomegranates, and nectarines. Even the buildings multiplied. Joe added a barn, a pool hall, storage sheds, chicken coops, and separate living quarters for workers. The homestead at 749 North Walnut became a successful ranch, and its inhabitants enjoyed an unusual lifestyle for a Sunland family.

Tony and Josephine play in their driveway. Behind them, a few roof tops peek above the sage brush in the far distance. Today that empty land is filled by the homes opposite Mt. Gleason Jr. High School.
Photo courtesy of Mrs. J. Kemp.

In 1930, with the renaming of streets, the address changed to 10949 Mt. Gleason Avenue, the future site of Mt. Gleason Junior High School. The 25-30 acre ranch seemed larger because relatives owned the surrounding property, including a water plant and pumping station which stood on the corner of Hillrose Street and Woodward Avenue. A reservoir full of clean water for irrigation tempted many local kids to sneak in for a swim.

Although a foreman, Gasparone ("Sponnie") Cacciatore, oversaw care of the vineyards and orchards of figs and plums as well as the running of the winery, life on the ranch kept Elsie very busy, especially after the birth of her children: Tony in 1917 and Josephine in 1919. Like most Sunland families, Elsie kept a vegetable garden, canned fruit, and made jelly. On weekends, the kids took advantage of their location on Walnut, the main route into Big Tujunga Canyon. Joe built a fruit stand in front of the house, from which they earned as much as $20 a day selling grapes, figs, and plums to passers-by on their way up the canyon. A large basket of grapes sold for 25 cents.

Sundays, the customary gathering day for Italian families, Elsie made tomato paste for the dinner sauce in a big wash tub with a screen for a strainer. Then, following tradition, the men made the sauce. Since the local Valley Center Market on Michigan Avenue (later Foothill

Boulevard) near Summitrose carried only a limited line of groceries, Joe did the 'big' shopping in downtown L.A. for fresh garlic and cheese, pepperoni, salami, anchovies, and other ingredients. The extended Ardizzone family enjoyed eating and singing or just sitting around the table sharing family news on those noisy Sundays.

And what's a ranch without its quota of animals: cows, goats, horses, an aviary with beautiful birds, and Elsie's three yards of chickens for eggs and meat—and a

Elsie, Tony, and Josephine, like other early Sunlanders, often traveled around town in a horse cart. Because of the rutted dirt roads, the going was bumpy and rather slow. Photo courtesy of the Ardizone family.

little amusement. One of the wooden tanks in the chicken yard, used to store the dregs of wine drained from the winery vats, dripped. The chickens loved to drink from the steady trickle of wine causing them to stagger around the yard afterward, much to the delight of the children.

Hay in the barn provided a breeding ground for cats, who often scratched the kids trying to play with the kittens. In the kennels out back, Joe and Elsie raised German shepherds. They gave many of the dogs away, but always kept a minimum of six to patrol at night between the chain link fence and the house. The shrubbery Joe loved and planted around the house obscured a clear view of the road, so the dogs provided protection against unseen enemies.

Elsie's hard work on the ranch did not prevent her from spending time with her children. She usually drove them the one mile back and forth to Sunland School on Hillrose in her Model T. At noon, she brought hot lunches in a picnic basket, and they would sit in the car under the shade of the trees to eat. Most of the school kids joined in playground games or tramped together down to the wash during lunch. Tony and Josephine did not join their classmates in such activities. Name-calling and nasty remarks about their Italian heritage hurt the children and segregated them somewhat from their classmates.

Although Elsie restricted her driving to town, she loved to drive. Any excuse would do to get in the car, including giving lots of rides. The kids particularly enjoyed excursions up Big Tujunga Canyon. While the adults sat inside the Model T, the kids stood on running boards and hung on. Each time they crossed the river, the water splashed across them, making the trip as much fun as the destination.

The same yard and house pictured on page ten
after Joe finished the landscaping and making other improvements.
Photo courtesy of the Ardizone family.

Mafia Connections

In addition to his role as rancher, by 1926, Joe Ardizzone officially served as treasurer of the Italian Protection League with Jack Dragna[4], president of the League and titular head of the Mafia in California. Most of the week, Joe worked at their offices in downtown Los Angles, but he often traveled to Chicago and New York to see Al Capone and other syndicate bosses. Unlike the early Mafia which formed to protect the poor and the weak, the Mafia had evolved into a criminal underworld. It should be noted that in the early 1900s, few, including the government, believed that the Mafia existed or understood its role in organized crime.

Whatever Joe's role and activities in the Mafia may have been, at home he was a good father and husband who treated his family, friends, and neighbors well. A cigar box full of IOUs attested to his generosity in lending money. He also gave supplies when needed. For example, when the neighboring Silva family experienced a period of financial problems, Joe bought food for the family and hay for the horses. Elsie dressed in the finest clothes, accented with lavish jewels. On his trips back East, he always remembered to send his children postcards and returned home laden with gifts of clothing and toys.

While Elsie had learned Italian very quickly, Joe often helped Tony and Josephine with their homework to perfect his English skills. Ironically, since both parents wanted to practice their second language, Joe insisted the children speak English with him, while Elsie insisted they speak Italian to her. Josephine didn't realize her mother wasn't Italian until she was 14.

Although Joe could be generous and affectionate, his children also knew his sterner side. He imposed strict rules, like not riding too far away from home on their bicycles, or always coming straight home from school. The sternness was a measure of protection, like the guard dogs. He knew, better than anyone, the potential danger his Mafia connections imposed on his children. He did not tolerate any backtalk from his children—or anyone else. No one crossed Joe Ardizzone, "Iron Man" of the Mafia.

When home, Joe hosted parties and entertained judges, senators, governors, and law enforcement officials. These well-dressed, affluent guests often gave ten-dollar gold pieces to Tony and Josephine. Fortunately, Elsie deposited the money in the bank; she would need it later. The family often dined at the home of John Steven McGroarty—

journalist, U.S. Congressman, and Poet Laureate of California, who also lived in town.[5] When McGroarty started his Mission Play about the early history of California, Joe rounded up friends and relatives from L.A. to pack the audience. Joe's support of the arts extended to helping several movie stars, including Rudolph Valentino.

Joe Ardizzone raised dogs to patrol the property at night.
Photo courtesy of Mrs. Josephine Kemp.

Every year the family vacationed for three weeks at Venice Beach, but never by themselves. Joe rented a large two-story 'mansion' and invited as many as 30 friends or relatives to share their vacation. Different groups came each year. The women and children stayed all week; children also enjoyed an extended stay at the ranch. The men came on weekends, when they seized the opportunity to visit the gambling boats moored out in international waters. Other vacations included car trips along terrible roads to San Francisco, Monterey, Carmel, and Ensenada, and boat trips to Catalina, Joe's favorite.

Joe loved gambling on horse and dog races, as did Elsie, who had her own bookie. At the ranch, both adults and kids played card games, especially poker, which Josephine learned to play at age five. When the adults played around the big dining-room table, they used coins instead of chips. The kids happily scrambled under the table to retrieve the coins dropped by enthusiastic players.

During Prohibition, Joe became heavily involved with bootlegging. Since he owned his own winery, he could grow grapes and process and bottle wine himself, although his still up in Big Tujunga Canyon was not actually on Ardizzone property. Secret tunnels under the house offered escape routes, underground passages into the vineyards, and access to three cellars for storing wine. One cellar was under the two-car garage, another under the house, and the largest out back, with a secret trap door in the closet of the foreman's house.

Official policy during Prohibition allowed wineries to continue making wine for personal consumption. Besides serving wine as a typical part of an Italian meal, during the summer, Elsie served lunch and dinner on their screened-in porch to the grape-pickers working in the vineyards. To retrieve cool pitchers of wine to serve with their meal, Elsie simply lifted the trap door next to the table on the porch to gain access to the wine cellar.

But not all the bottles of wine Joe produced could be considered 'for personal consumption.' He also supplied wine and other types of liquor to outsiders. Using the secret tunnels to access the property around the still, Joe hid bottles in the rock wall and cactus which his customers retrieved from their hiding places. When Mt. Gleason Junior High was constructed, tractors kept sinking into the old tunnels. The builders finally contacted Tony to pinpoint the location of the tunnels so they could avoid further accidents.

As a Mafia boss, Joe tried to 'muscle in' on other bootlegging and smuggling businesses. A gang war started during an argument between Joe and two bootleggers from 'Little Italy' in Los Angeles. In February, 1931, Joe invited

Jimmy Basile, one of those bootleggers, for a 'ride.' Basile's friends saw Jimmy in Downey with Joe and opened fire on the car. Joe crawled away, wounded but alive. Jimmy did not fare as well—he was caught in the crossfire. While Joe battled with local rivals, he also quarreled with Eastern interests trying to 'muscle in' on him.

Joe disrupted the status quo of the Mafia and made enemies. While he recuperated at Hollywood Presbyterian Hospital, his brothers and nephews took turns as armed guards and foiled a second attempt on his life. As an extra precaution, Joe wouldn't eat the hospital food; a personal cook brought his lunch and dinner.

His youngest sister, Christina, nicknamed Tini because of her diminutive four-foot-eleven inches and size-four shoe, constantly worried and warned Joe. "They're after you," she'd say, or "Don't go by yourself." Although he carried a Colt revolver in the car on the seat next to him, Joe seemed more concerned with his family's safety than his own.

One day after stopping at the library, Tony and Josephine arrived home later than usual. Elsie loved to read to the children and passed on her love for books. They enjoyed such classics as *Heidi, Little Women, Anne of Green Gables, Nancy Drew mysteries, Tom Swift,* and *Tarzan.* With their mother's permission, they stopped at the one-room library near Fenwick and Floralita after school to return and borrow books. This day, however, their father came home from work very early. Furious, fearful for their safety, he lashed at them verbally, insisting they never go alone again, but just come straight home from school. Too bad Joe didn't listen to his own advice.

In that simpler time, parents didn't have to teach kids lessons like "Don't take rides from strangers." But Tony and Josephine did not live the ordinary life of other Sunland kids. Perhaps her father's fear had communicated itself in more ways than just words. One day a stranger stopped Josephine as she was walking home. Scared, she ran the rest of the way, realizing her father would have killed the man if he had witnessed the incident. And she was quite literally correct. The "Iron Man" supposedly admitted to killing 30 unwilling business associates as he threatened the 31st.[6]

On October 15, 1931[7], Joe left home at 6:30 a.m. for a short trip to a ranch near Ettiwanda to pick up a relative. Hopefully, he kissed his wife and children fondly in parting, for they would never see him again. The man and his automobile simply disappeared into history. For weeks, the police searched for clues, but to no avail. At the time, Elsie was 33, Tony 14, and Josephine 11. Joe was officially declared dead seven years later.

The Ardizzones -- Joe, Tony, Elsie, and Josephine -- at their home on Mt. Gleason Avenue. Photo courtesy of the Ardizone family.

Life after Joe

Elsie's life changed once more. No more fine clothes or lavish jewels. No more large parties, elegant dinners, or oceanside vacations. No more 'friends' from other Mafia families who immediately severed all ties with her. She'd lost her husband and her security, but not her pioneer spirit.

Joe's disappearance during the Great Depression compounded Elsie's predicament. The cigar box of promissory notes from people who owed Joe thousands and thousands of dollars proved to be valueless when they failed to repay the loans. Whether they couldn't or wouldn't is irrelevant; the fact is, they didn't. When so many people lived on the edge of starvation, few had the resources to reach out to Elsie and her children. Only her sister Frances and her brother-in-law Cecil came faithfully once a week with groceries or clothes for the kids.

Without help, except for their faithful foreman, Sponnie, who stayed on without pay, Elsie survived on her own ingenuity. She fought to keep the ranch by marketing homemade wine, and selling off furniture, winery equipment, and rooms full of tools. Because of the Depression, they sold for a fraction of their value. She rented the extra house, formerly for workers, for income. In spite of her efforts, she lost the battle with the mortgage two years later and moved to 10610 Pinyon Street in Tujunga, while Josephine attended high school in San Fernando. Later, she moved again to 10407 Eldora Street in Sunland.

Just before he disappeared, Joe had given Tony a new Ford Cabriolet convertible. Joe surprised his kids by picking them up from school on Tony's birthday. As they turned into the driveway lined with lots of friends and relatives, a band started playing. There in the driveway, decorated with ribbons, waited Tony's present. At the time, the Ardizzones had four other cars: a Lincoln, two Fords, and a truck. Elsie sold these, and when they moved to Pinyon Street, aside from being a fond memory of Joe, Tony's car provided their sole means of transportation.

Never embittered by her tragic loss, Elsie remained sociable and friendly, her home open to her friends and those of her children. The kids hosted many a party; they'd roll up the rug in the big living room and dance to the music from their record player—one of the last gifts from their father. When a new family moved into the neighborhood several houses down, Elsie insisted

Josephine go welcome the daughter and bring the girl back to join the fun.

Elsie worked at the Wooden Rattler Restaurant on the corner of Mt. Gleason and Foothill. Joe originally constructed the building in 1929 as a fruit stand. When that didn't work, it became a soda fountain, an ice house, and finally a restaurant. Fortunately, Elsie retained title to the property when the bank foreclosed on the ranch. Elsie and her boyfriend Patty McMann took over the restaurant which gained popularity with Elsie's famous French dip sandwiches and hamburgers, and they added a beer and wine bar.

Tony's Café has changed hands several times over the years.

After years of staying at home, Elsie loved her new role. "When she got out and went to work at that bar, it was just like a new life for her. She met a lot of people, and they all loved her. She'd rather be there than anywhere else."[8]

On Your Way to or From The

OLD TIMERS CELEBRATION
STOP OFF AT ...

T O N Y'S

"For Short Orders That
Are Hard to Beat ...

... and
C O C K T A I L S
Like "Old Timers Make!"

Foothill at Mt. Gleason
Sunland, Calif.   Florida 3-9915

Advertisement in The Record-Ledger 7/28/55

**The Old Timers Celebration was an annual event of spoof
and fun commemorating Sunland's origin.**

In the late 1940s, her son Tony took over the restaurant and renamed it Tony's Café. Until 1967, Elsie remained as the official manager, cooking and ordering supplies for her son. As the city widened Foothill Boulevard and Mt. Gleason Avenue, it sliced off pieces of the property until the sidewalks crept right up to the sides of the building. In the 1970s, Tony's Café sold. It has changed ownership several times since, functioning as a cocktail lounge.

Socially, Elsie remained very active. She participated in the Foothill Funsters, enjoyed trips to Las Vegas, the horse races, and an occasional toddy. At home she enjoyed playing the piano and raising African violets. Personally she remained very disciplined, running her life on a schedule, and always dressed stylishly, complete with scarf and gloves.

Elsie Elizabeth Ellenberg Ardizzone died on March 5, 1987, at the age of 89. With her died an unusual chapter in the history of Sunland.

#####

Footnotes

[1]   This was probably part of the land brought by Hartranft in 1907 and subdivided into plots of 5, 10, and 20 acres.

[2]   Joe's son Tony later changed the spelling of the family name to Ardizone, with one z. Early records use two z's so that is the spelling used when appropriate.

[3]   *The Grim Reapers*, pp. 3-4.

[4]   Jack Dragna's real name was Anthony Rizzoti. He came from Corleone, Sicily, in 1908.

[5]   McGroarty's home became the McGroarty Arts Center, 7570 McGroarty Terrace, Tujunga.

[6]   *The Grim Reapers*, p. 165.

[7]   Joe's disappearance coincided with Al Capone's trial for tax evasion. Capone was convicted two days after Joe disappeared on October 17, 1931.

[8]   Personal interview with Josephine Kemp by Mary Lee Tiernan. July 19, 1999.

Bibliography

"Ardizzone Case Report Denied." *The Los Angeles Times*, October 20, 1931.

Ardizone, Caroline. Personal interview by Mary Lou Pozzo. November 1, 1997.

Ardizone, Caroline. Personal interview by Mary Lou Pozzo. April 25, 1998.

"Bootleg Gangs Open New War." *The Los Angeles Times*, October 18, 1931.

"Fire Destroys House Owned by Joe Ardizzone." *The Record-Ledger*, Thursday, March 19, 1924.

Hartranft, Edward. Personal Interview. March 30, 1974.

Kemp, Josephine (Ardizone). Personal interview by Mary Lee Tiernan. July 19, 1999.

Reid, Ed. *The Grim Reapers: The Anatomy of Organized Crime in America.* Chicago: Henry Regnery Company, 1969.

"Salvatore Ardizzone, Early Valley Settler, Farmer, Dies at Age 79." *The Record-Ledger*, Thursday, March 27, 1958.

"Search Futile for Ardizzone." *The Los Angeles Times*, October 21, 1931.

"Winery Found in Haystacks." *The Los Angeles Times*, October 24, 1931.

Lancasters Lake

The quaint little lake on Sherman Grove Avenue cast on a spell on all who visited its shores, including some Hollywood stars.

The Early History of Sunland, California
Volume 6

ML Tiernan

When Edgar Lancaster dredged the swamp on his land, he created a lake which became a treasured landmark. For 25 years, visitors flocked to its cool shores, and Hollywood used the lake as a set location for some of its early movies.

Lancasters Lake

The swamp that grew into one of Sunland's treasured landmarks.

**The Early History of Sunland, California
Volume 6**

ML Tiernan

Lancasters Lake

www.maryleetiernan.com
Second printing April 1, 2015
10 9 8 7 6 5 4 3 2

ISBN 978-0983067252 (Paperback)

Photograph on cover courtesy of Bolton Hall Museum, Tujunga, California.

Contents

The Family

With only a dozen or so families living in Sunland, the addition of six more people named Lancaster shouldn't have posed a problem. So when Margaret sent her youngsters off to school, she probably looked forward to a day of unpacking without her four children underfoot. How much easier that would be! Imagine her astonishment

The Lancasters' first home on Sherman Grove Avenue circa 1922.
Photo courtesy of Marshall Murray.

when William, Paul, Marie, and Irene appeared back home only minutes later. The tiny, one-room schoolhouse had no room for them.

The arrival of the Lancaster family foreshadowed many changes for Sunland. The first, obviously, was to enlarge the schoolhouse an additional six feet to accommodate the new attendees. But what if other new students needed to be squeezed in? An extension only offered a temporary solution.

The need for a newer and larger school spawned Edgar Lancaster's leadership. He headed a movement to build one, and despite the opposition, he won. The next year, the new school, located on the northeast corner of Sunland Park, easily accommodated all the children in its one large room.

Edgar Lancaster had operated a grocery store in Pasadena for many years. Customers normally paid for groceries by credit, not cash, by entering their names in a book on the counter. Fed up with trying to collect over-due bills, Edgar sold the store and initially bought five acres of land in Sunland just north of the park, on the west side of Sherman Grove Avenue. The purchase included a house, an orchard, a swamp, and enough pasture for a cow, horses, chickens, ducks, and a couple of hogs.

Edgar continued in the grocery business, but now as a

farmer, growing and selling the fruit from his orchard. Each day he drove fourteen miles to Pasadena to take his peaches to market, a trip that took three hours each way along a one-lane dirt road. Later the family bought an additional 20 acres, full of weeds and dead grapevines, east of Oro Vista and south of Foothill. After reviving the vineyard, Edgar or his son Paul delivered both grapes and peaches to the Pasadena markets. The trip improved after 1910, when the county paved the dirt road—then called Michigan Avenue, later renamed Foothill Boulevard—and widened it to 15 feet.

Edgar began digging out a swampy portion of his land.
Photo courtesy of Bolton Hall Museum.

Few businesses existed in Sunland when the Lancasters moved there, simply because not enough people lived in the valley to support many stores. And everyone attended the Free Methodist Church, the only church in town—until the arrival of the Lancasters, that is. When it came to attending Sunday school, Bill Lancaster protested. Attending a Methodist Sunday school didn't bother his Baptist upbringing; no, he refused on the basis that "only girls went there,"[1] and he wasn't going to get caught with just a bunch of girls.

Instead of arguing with him, Margaret and Edgar sent him out to round up his friends. That afternoon, the Lancasters held their own Sunday school with 11 boys in the front room of their home. The next Sunday, 29 people attended. Thus the Lancasters brought the Baptist Church to Sunland.

By the next year, the Sunday school outgrew the Lancaster living room and moved into the new schoolhouse for meetings. As the congregation expanded over the next ten years, the need for a church of their own became evident. Edgar and Dr. G.M. Hammond donated land on Eldora for the building of the Sunland Baptist Church, erected in 1925. But as pleased as the members were about their new church, they thought longingly of the one thing it lacked because the cost of building the church had depleted their fund. They wanted a bell.

Many of the movie studios filmed in and around Sunland in those early days. Abe Lincoln strode through Sunland Park[2], Zorro raced down Roscoe Boulevard[3], and

Claudette Colbert raised her skirt a few inches to hitch a ride[4], a provocative action at the time. The Lancasters became acquainted with yet another star, Mary Pickford, as several of her films were shot on their land. Grateful to the Lancasters for their hospitality, she graciously donated the bell for the new church. When the congregation moved to another location on Oro Vista in 1951, they brought the bell with them. It rang on Sunday mornings—once to signal the beginning of worship, and once more to signal the end.

Fishing on the lake - probably in the late 1920s.
Photo courtesy of Bolton Hall Museum.

The Lancaster home was typical of early Sunland: a fireplace for heat, kerosene lamps for light, a well for running water. Fruit from the orchard was eaten fresh, in season, or canned; family gardens provided vegetables. For meat, the menfolk might venture into the nearby hills and hunt, and mom usually raised poultry in the backyard. In a pinch, one could buy meat from the butcher who came to town once a week.

Although one could go to Los Angeles for needed supplies, the long trip precluded their going very often. For the most part, these self-reliant pioneers produced what they needed themselves, whether in terms of goods or know-how. For example, when electricity arrived in 1914, no utility truck pulled up in front to hookup the house to the lines. Residents installed their own wiring, which usually ran helter-skelter across the land. During inclement weather, the wiring often broke and residents followed the lines to locate the problems and make their own repairs.

1927 - early days at the lake. Photo courtesy of Marshall Murray.

Neighbors and family just naturally helped each other. It's hard to imagine that a half-hour car trip (traffic permitting) to Los Angeles in modern times took two days by horse in the early 1900s. When Clara and Alfred Blumfield, who lived across the street from the Lancasters, needed to go "to town," Margaret automatically invited their children into her home. She would later have to do the same for her own grandchildren.

During the devastating flu pandemic of 1918-1919, which affected 25 percent of the U.S. population and killed 20 million people world-wide, Margaret's daughter Irene and her husband Ivan both caught the flu. Irene and Ivan lived near Irene's sister Marie in Jerome, Arizona. When their baby, also named Irene, was only six weeks old, her

**The northern end of the lake when one could
drive up to the picnic area.**

Aunt Marie brought her to California so her grandparents could care for her. To keep the baby safe during the train trip, Marie kept the baby in a picnic basket. That almost had the opposite effect, however, when a well-intentioned man tried to grab the basket as Marie struggled to board the train. "Be careful," she yelled, "there's a baby in there."[5] Mother Irene "went to meet the Lord," as brother Paul expressed it, but Ivan eventually recovered and later remarried.

All the children helped out with typical chores like milking the cows or feeding the chickens. Marie's contribution may have been the most unique. She gave English lessons two nights a week to five or six Japanese workers who picked olives in the Wright groves.

After her divorce in 1934, daughter Marie returned to Sunland with her children to live with Granpa[6] Lancaster. And the chores were still there—this time for the grandchildren—and this time at the lake.

"I was put in charge of the boats," said Marshall Murray. "I had to collect 35 cents for 30 minutes of rental time, call the boats in if they failed to come in on time, breakup water fights, and keep general law and order."[7] The hardest part, he admitted, was having to work when his friends came to the lake to play.

After eighth grade, the Lancaster children attended

Glendale High School. By 1913, an electric car ran between Glendale and Montrose. The kids caught a bus from Sunland to the end of the line in Montrose, took the electric car to Glendale, and caught another bus to the high school, usually getting there on time. When Paul graduated in 1917, eight Sunland students made this daily trip.

The long hours traveling back and forth to school and the chores at home didn't prevent the youngsters from enjoying themselves. Paul Lancaster and Elmer Adams liked to pile loose hay high on a big flat-top truck drawn by horses. They packed some picnic baskets, picked up friends and neighbors, and headed out for a day of fun. Inventive as their parents, someone usually brought along a homemade ukulele crafted from a wooden cigar box to accompany the singing. Four rubber bands, fastened with tacks, stretched across the length of the box for strings; a piece of straight wood formed the neck. And it did the job quite well.

At other times, the kids amused themselves with ice cream socials, rabbit hunting, Sunday school parties, corn roasts, taffy pulls, potato bakes, or plays in the park. And they didn't spend much time on the phone, especially since one line served the entire town and anyone could pick up the phone and listen in on their conversations.

The entrance to Lancasters Lake on Sherman Grove Avenue circa 1937 driving north from Sunland Park toward Wentworth Avenue.

Photo courtesy of Marshall Murray.

The Lake

The 1920s brought bobbed hair, the Charleston, and fringed flapper dresses to the rest of the world; to Sunland they brought Lancasters Lake.[8] After the death of his wife Margaret, or Maggie, in October 1922, Edgar was so depressed that he wanted to leave the ranch and never return. He traveled north to visit some of the wonders of the West, including Crater Lake. He did return to Sunland,

The lake circa 1931. Photo courtesy of Bolton Hall Museum.

but he was lonely and restless. His grandson Marshall Murray recalls, "He wanted something—something big and important. Crater Lake gave him the inspiration to make a lake from the wet area on the ranch. He thought that if he could scoop the mud out of the wet hollow, he might pump in enough water to fill up the hole and make a lake."[9]

Without the benefit of bulldozers or other mechanical diggers, early settlers scooped out the earth the hard way while clearing building sites. Along with the earth came the never-ending supply of rocks. These thrifty founders piled the rocks as berms for strong foundations or retaining walls, or constructed homes. Many of these original buildings and berms are still standing.

The museum housed an assortment of relics from pioneer days.
Photo courtesy of Marshall Murray.

On hot summer days, the children in town begged to go swimming in the new lake and the accommodating Lancasters consented. Girls could swim two days a week, boys the rest of the time, with a family member acting as lifeguard.

A solid rock hill north of Sunland Park, which prevented water run-off from draining into the ground, had originally created the wet hollow or swamp on the back of the Lancaster property. After Edgar's excavation, in addition to the water he pumped into the lake, water continued to seep naturally into the basin, filling it up, and

One of the cabins at the lake available for rent.
Photo courtesy of Marshall Murray.

Edgar kept digging it out. By 1924, the rustic lake covered two acres with a depth of about four feet.

Because of the muddy bottom, the lake was no longer suitable for swimming, although the kids "just sort of fell in"[10] when the hot sun blazed. Sunland Park remained the more popular spot for family picnics and outings, but the lake definitely attracted the kids who "went and hoped

The "snack shack" sold treats such as soda or ice cream but was also the place to rent a boat or a fishing pole.
Photo courtesy of Marshall Murray.

something fun happened."[11] For 25 years, locals and visitors flocked to it cool shores for a day of relaxation or adventure.

Edgar "Granpa" Lancaster
Photos courtesy of Marshall Murray.

The children's special playground with Edgar's handcarved animals to ride and miniature merry-go-rounds made from wagon wheels.

Most of the animals had leather ears and saddle,
a rope tail, a moveable head, and pop-bottle eyes.

Just opposite where Hillrose Street once dead-ended into 10711 Sherman Grove Avenue, two tall poles, standing at an angle from the road, marked the entrance to Lancasters Lake. Up the short, curved path on the left stood a small museum, constructed from rock. It housed discarded implements used by Sunland's earliest founders, wooden Indians carved by Edgar, an old pump organ, pachinko games, horse livery, old clothes, and movie memorabilia including an old-time moving-picture machine where one flipped individual pictures to make them 'move.' The windows, made from wagon wheels with colored glass inserted between the spokes, showered the inside of the museum with magical color. The contents of the museum 'disappeared' during the 1950s when the land was leased. Beyond the museum stood two or three small, picturesque cabins.

Young children dashed toward their own special play area on the right, with swings and miniature merry-go-rounds made from wagon wheels. The wheels were mounted on posts firmly planted in the ground. The kids sat on the wheels, held on to the spokes, and used their feet to spin the wheel round and round till they grew dizzy. For their pleasure, Edgar also carved animals from logs, the wood soon worn smooth from the loving touch of many small hands. Whether a rocking horse, buffalo, pig, elephant, or camel, each had leather ears and saddle, a rope tail, a moveable head, and pop-bottle eyes.

"Granpa Lancaster," as the children called him, may have been physically small in stature, but not in his love for children. Summer crowds at the lake thinned during the winter, so it was not too unusual to have the lake to oneself, especially on an overcast day. One of the children, who lived close by, decided to take her new puppy down to the lake to treat him to a ride in a rowboat. Only the puppy saw a squirrel and got so excited that he jumped up and down, tipping over the boat. When Granpa Lancaster came to the rescue, the child tearfully pleaded, "Please, don't tell my mother."[12] Edgar took the child into the snack shack, warmed up the old wood stove, and let child and puppy dry out before he sent them on their way. And he never did tell.

One reached the longer section of the lake first. At the very end, the picnic area included a pavilion, reminiscent of a little stage, used by one of the movie studios as a set for a fight scene in a Joe Lewis movie. Those interested in rowing or fishing walked north on the right side of the lake to rent a boat or a fishing pole at the snack shack, or treated themselves to soda-pop or ice cream. Edgar added rowboats to the lake in 1926; he named the original six after his grandchildren. Rowers guided the blue and green boats around the lake and under the arched stone bridge on the north end into a lagoon. The less ambitious just rowed out to the middle of the lake and drifted lazily, or settled back and cast their fishing lines.

The boats also tempted local boys who liked to play a harmless prank. Before the lake would open for the day, they would row the boats out to the tiny island on the south end of the lake and beach them, knowing full well that Paul Lancaster, pretending to be irate, would then come chasing after them with his shotgun.

The pavilion on the south end of the lake was used as a movie set.

The cattails growing around the lake prompted another prank when movie director D.W. Griffith was filming in

Sunland Park. Some of the boys gathered the cattails and brought them to the park where they pulled them, filling the air with slow-floating fluff. A furious Griffith had to "cut" and wait for the air to clear before he could resume filming.

In 1927, the Lancasters seeded the lake with 500 catfish. Visitors could rent a simple fishing pole: a long pole, sans reel, with bait attached on the end of the line. Tom Sawyer would have felt right at home. Catfish cost 25¢ for each one caught.

Lush weeping willows and lilies surrounded the shorter section of the lake, creating a lagoon. The setting also attracted movie studios that filmed at this cherished community spot, which is how the Lancasters came to know Mary Pickford. While filming at the lake, studios usually setup tents for the stars who welcomed visits from the local kids. A friendly Alan Ladd invited the kids into his tent for a chat, and Forest Tucker let the kids try on his diving helmet, a prop for a "deep-sea" movie. They couldn't move under the weight of the old-fashioned helmet.

Visitors relaxed at the picnic tables carved from tree trunks. They could simply sit back and watch swans glide gracefully across the water, or wave to friends out rowing, or wander down to the water's edge to feed the ducks. To the delight of birdwatchers, the luxurious greenery attracted 51 different species of birds. Those looking for some exercise walked around the lake on a dirt path—well, almost around the lake. The many trees and plants bordering the lagoon hindered clear passage, so walkers usually by-passed the lagoon by crossing over the bridge. Eucalyptus trees shaded the north portion of the lake. Hidden among the trees on the west side, a creek ran through a ravine, a spot that local children found especially enticing.

An unusual storm covered Sunland in snow and froze the lake in January 1949.
Photo courtesy of Marshall Murray.

Perhaps the greatest attraction to local children was simply that the lake was there. It was their playground. If they didn't go the lake with friends, they went alone—someone they knew was sure to show up. If they didn't have the price of a rowboat or fishing pole, catching a polliwog was just as much fun. The ravine in back provided endless hours of exploring; the tiny island a perfect setting for playing marooned or Treasure Island. What their imaginations didn't supply, sometimes the movie studios did with their sets and stars—like Johnny Weissmuller fighting alligators by the bridge in one of his Tarzan movies.

Hollywood stars, however, can also deliver a harsh dose of reality. Marshall Murray recalls watching the filming of Tarzan. "I remember standing on the bridge that separated the two parts of the lake watching Tarzan stab an alligator with a rubber knife. A movie man saw me and said, 'Beat it, kid, you don't belong here.' I shouted back, 'I live here.' Johnny came out of the water wet and cold, and someone handed him a bottle of brandy. He took a couple of long drinks—there went my image of Tarzan!"[13]

The 25-year history of Lancasters Lake records only one disaster. Six-year-old Robert Lee Glover of Russett Avenue, Sunland, drowned in the lake in 1944, just a few years before the demise of the lake itself.

The construction of concrete drainage ditches from

Haines Canyon to the wash prevented water from seeping into the soil—water which had fed the lake. For a while, the family continued to pump water into the lake, but this, too, became a problem because the Adams Olive Cannery used water from the same pump, and there just wasn't enough water for both of them.

The bridge separated the two sections of the lake.
Photo courtesy of Bolton Hall Museum.

When Edgar had a stroke in 1949 and his grandson Marshall left for college, there was no one to care for the property. The water receded in the lake until it finally dried up around 1950. Health officials condemned the site as a breeding ground for mosquitoes and required the bed of the lake to be filled in. The demise of the lake foreshadowed that of its creator, Edgar Lancaster, who died in 1951 at the age of 93.

The Lancaster land was leased for a few years in the early 1950s. In 1954, John and Florence Plemmons bought it and renamed the site the Sherman Grove Park. Picnic grounds covered the old bed of the lake. Later the property was converted to the Sherman Grove Mobile Home Park, and the picnic tables became rows of house trailers.

#####

Map of Lancasters Lake

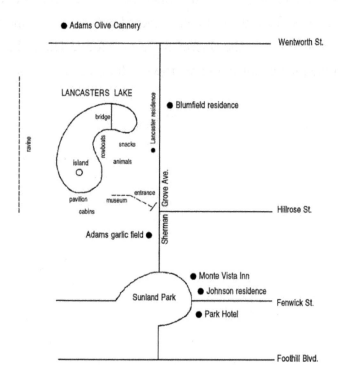

● Adams Olive Cannery

Wentworth St.

LANCASTERS LAKE

Lancaster residence

● Blumfield residence

bridge

rowboats

snacks

island

animals

pavilion

museum

entrance

cabins

Grove Ave.

Sherman

ravine

Adams garlic field ●

Hillrose St.

● Monte Vista Inn

● Johnson residence

Sunland Park

Fenwick St.

● Park Hotel

Foothill Blvd.

Footnotes

[1] "Sunland Baptists Celebrate 46-Year Growth with Dedication of New Church This Sunday," *The Record-Ledger*, January 27, 1955.

[2] D.W. Griffith's *Abraham Lincoln*.

[3] *The Mark of Zorro* with Douglas Fairbanks.

[4] *It Happened One Night*, also starring Clark Cable.

[5] Murray, Marshall. Letter to Mary Lee Tiernan.

[6] Spelling of 'grandpa' used for Edgar.

[7] Murray, Marshall. Letter to Mary Lee Tiernan.

[8] In popular parlance, the lake was often referred to as Lancaster Lake—no 's'. The Lancasters, however, called the lake Lancasters Lake—with an 's,' but no apostrophe. The second edition defers to the family's spelling.

[9] Murray, Marshall. Letter to Mary Lee Tiernan.

[10] Wheeler, Sherrie. Personal interview.

[11] Gillan, Norman. Personal interview.

[12] Wheeler, Sherrie. Personal interview.

[13] Murray, Marshall. Letter to Mary Lee Tiernan.

Bibliography

"Baptist Church in Sunland Inspired by Boy's Defiance." *The Record-Ledger*, Historical & Progress Edition, May 21, 1953.

"Boating Is Good at Lancaster's Lake." *The Record-Ledger*, July 29, 1926.

"Church Bell Given by Mary Pickford." *The Record-Ledger*, January 27, 1955.

Coronado, Addie. Personal interview by Mary Lee Tiernan. July 16, 1999.

"Death Takes E.F. Lancaster, Valley Pioneer." *The Glendale NewsPress*, July 20, 1951.

"Early History of Sunland Baptist Church." Clippings file, Special Collections, Glendale Public Library.

"Early Sunland Landmark." Clippings file, Bolton Hall Museum.

"Edgar Lancaster Celebrates 90th Birthday." *The Record-Ledger*, October 28, 1948.

"Excavating for Sunland Church." *The Record-Ledger*, February 21, 1924.

Gillan, Norman. Personal interview by Mary Lee Tiernan. July 17, 1999.

Glover, Robert Lee. Funeral record. Bade Mortuary, Tujunga, CA.

Harn, Jay. "He Was Here in the Beginning." *The Record-Ledger*, February 12, 1986.

Hitt, Marlene. "Lancaster Lake the Best Place to Spend a Hot Summer Day." *The Foothill Leader*, March 14-15, 1998.

"Lancaster Lake." *The Record-Ledger*, Historical & Progress Edition, May 21, 1953.

"Lancaster Lake Is Now Sherman Grove Park." *The Record-Ledger*, September 30, 1954.

Lancaster Paul. Personal interview by Charles Miller, August 16, 1986.

"Many People Visit Lancaster Lake on the Fourth of July." *The Record-Ledger*, July 7, 1933.

"Marie Murray Recalls Days of Father's Lancaster Lake." *The Record-Ledger*, September 30, 1954.

McKee, Bob. "Sunland Recalled." *The Record-Ledger*, July 24, 1976.

Monroe, Irene. Personal interview by Mary Lee Tiernan. July 20, 1999.

Murray, Marshall. Letter to Mary Lee Tiernan. March 28, 2000.

Pozzo, Mary Lou. *Hollywood Comes to Sunland-Tujunga 1920-1995.* Tujunga, CA: Sunland-Tujunga Little Landers Historical Society. 1995.

Schell, Elizabeth Blumfield. "Early Memories of My Childhood." July 24, 1983.

"Sunland Baptists Celebrate 46-Year Growth with Dedication of New Church This Sunday." *The Record-Ledger*, January 27, 1955.

"Sunland School Nears 70 Years at Same Site." *The Record-Ledger*, July 3, 1975.

Sunland-Tujunga: Nestled between the Verdugo Hills and the San Gabriel Mts. The Sunland-Tujunga Chamber of Commerce. March, 1947.

Wheeler, Sherrie. Personal interview by Mary Lee Tiernan. July 28, 1999.

"Will Build Camp at Sunland." *The Record-Ledger*, August 6, 1925.

"Will Hold Picnic at Lancaster Lake." *The Record-Ledger*, August 19, 1926.

Wollard, Jack. Personal interview by Mary Lee Tiernan. July 17, 1999.

Living in
Big Tujunga Canyon

**"The Gabrielinos looked upon the mountains
with a deep spiritual reverence."
Then came the white man...**

The Early History of Sunland, California
Volume 7

ML Tiernan

Early settlers, like the Johnson family, found their way into the canyon, a dense woodland bristling with wildlife. 50 years later, the Webber family faced the wrath of the river now winding down a denuded mountainside.

Living in Big Tujunga Canyon

*She nurtured life with water and woods,
then with angry, thundering waves,
washed it away.*

**The Early History of Sunland, California
Volume 7**

ML Tiernan

Living in Big Tujunga Canyon

www.maryleetiernan.com
Second printing April 1, 2015
10 9 8 7 6 5 4 3 2

ISBN 978-0983067269 (Paperback)

Photograph on the cover courtesy of Bolton Hall Museum, Tujunga, California.
Quote on the cover is from John W. Robinson's *The San Gabriels*, p. 5.

Contents

In the Beginning...

In days past, Big Tujunga Canyon bristled with life. Grizzly bears roamed through forests of live oak, cottonwood, walnut, alder, and willow trees. Seeds, animals, and birds traveled from the desert in the north through the canyon to the southern slopes. In the wash—a flood plain about a quarter of a mile wide at the base of the canyon—the seeds rooted and thrived, offering a unique blend of brush and wildlife from different climatic zones.

Big Tujunga Canyon and Wash. Photo courtesy of Bruce Perry.

Through it all, the river flowed freely, bringing its life-sustaining nourishment.

The denuding of the canyon began in the early 1800s with the building of the San Fernando Mission, which needed lumber for its construction and grazing land for its large herds of cattle. The padres lost their rights to the mission lands only decades later when the Mexican government, which ruled California, secularized the land in 1833 and redistributed it as land grants.

In 1840, brothers Francisco and Pedro Lopez were given part of the former San Fernando Mission lands to raise cattle. On their Rancho Tujunga, vaqueros herded cattle and horses far into the mouth of Big Tujunga Canyon with its abundant supply of chaparral and water. The discovery of the Lopez documents ended the once-popular belief that the Verdugo family land grant which encompassed parts of Glendale, La Crescenta, and La Canada had also included the Sunland-Tujunga area.

With the ranches and horses came the horse thieves. In the dense woodlands of the canyons, many a bandit hid from the law. The notorious Tiburcio Vasquez used the San Gabriel Mountains as his hideout for more than 20 years. During his last escapade in April 1874, he eluded capture by climbing into the mountains near La Canada, crossing through Vasquez Canyon to the Big Tujunga, then slipping down the Big Tujunga Canyon, or the BT in local parlance, to the valley. Vasquez Canyon's name recalls that last dramatic getaway.

Big Tujunga provided timber for many a long-gone cabin or hacienda. The rapidly growing city of Los Angeles needed wood, lots of wood. To satisfy this hunger for fuel and building materials, woodcutters cut down the oak and pine trees growing in abundance along the fringes of the mountains and in the canyon and then hauled the logs by horse and

Big Tujunga Canyon

wagon down the valley through Glendale. Many of their paths became the early roads in the valley.

While the woodcutters stripped the canyon of trees, hundreds of prospectors flocked to the BT in the 1870s and 1880s after the discovery of gold. They mined the earth for placer gold and the richer gold-bearing quartz until the craze for gold sent them after the next strike. While they plundered the earth beneath the canyon's surface, hunters and fishermen arrived in larger and larger numbers to kill the canyon's wildlife for sport. Bear, mountain lions, and deer, as well as smaller game, fell to the bang of a gun.

The lands surrounding the canyon attracted farmers who tilled the fertile land, rich from soil washed down the mountain. Some like Pedro Ybarra came to farm; some like Farmer Johnson came as woodcutters, but stayed to ranch. Others like Sherman Page and F.C. Howes came to cash in on the land boom and build a town.[1]

And so the white man began to inhabit the lands where the Gabrielino Indians had walked for thousands of years. A branch of the Gabrielinos—the Tuhunga Indians—had settled in the distant past in the region near Hansen Dam. Older documents refer to Lake View Terrace as Tuhunga Valley because of its proximity to the original village of the Tuhungas, not to be confused with the much later city of Tujunga to the east.

The exact meaning of the name Tuhunga is lost in time. For some, it comes from an old Gabrielino word meaning 'place of the old woman,' suggesting a tribute to Mother Earth and to the bounty of the canyon. Some claim the word means 'big thunder,' aptly named for those times when Mother Earth sends boulders and swollen flood waters crashing down the canyon. From the time the Lopez brothers established their rancho, spelling variations of *Tejunga* or *Tujunga* or even *Tijunga* began to appear. The more commonly used *Tujunga* became the accepted spelling.

Whatever the original name meant or the variations in spelling, the duality of the canyon challenged those who chose to live there. They traded enjoyment of its beauty for harsh living conditions—especially from flood waters tearing down the mountainside and washing out roads, leaving them isolated on the mountain. Man may borrow the canyon, but he will never tame her.

Sunland Park in the 1880-1890s

Early Sunland
Photos courtesy of Bolton Hall Museum.

Early Homesteaders

Cornelius and Alice Johnson wound their way over the rough ground, thick with bushes. Their footsteps obliterated those left by the deer on the narrow trail to Big Tujunga Canyon. The afternoon sun warmed their backs on that fall afternoon in 1916[2] as they bent to clear brush from the entrance of the canyon basin. Like the Gabrielino

Villagers took turns posing with the grizzly.
Photo courtesy of Bolton Hall Museum.

Indians who'd lived there for centuries past, the Johnsons knew that clearing the trail kept the canyon passable and helped prevent the spread of forest fires.

Spotting some unusual tracks on the soft ground, Alice called to her husband. Cornelius joined her and bent down to examine the earth. To his surprise, he recognized the imprints as bear tracks. While grizzlies had once freely roamed the canyons, most had disappeared as man settled in. Knowing the grizzly could be vicious, Cornelius took Alice safely home. He grabbed his shotgun and returned to search the area, but did not see the bear.

A few days later, Cornelius found evidence of the bear feeding on the lower section of the ranch. Honey from their beehives and the ripe fruit still hanging on their trees attracted the bear and would keep it in the vicinity. Fearful for his seven-year-old daughter Lucille who walked to school through this section of the ranch, Cornelius set a trap and lashed it to a log.

When Cornelius checked the next morning, both trap and log had disappeared. He tracked the bear by following the thrashed brush all the way up the mountain. Worn out from fighting the log he dragged with him, the bear, still caught in the trap, collapsed when the log jammed between two trees. Without hesitation, Cornelius aimed his 30-30 and shot the bear once behind the ear. Newspapers would later call it the $1,000 shot, claiming the rare silvertip grizzly would have been worth $1,000 or more if taken alive.[3]

News of the kill spread quickly. Neighbors arrived to help chain the 300 pound carcass to a pole and bring it down the mountain to the community's central gathering place, Sunland Park. An unofficial holiday ensued. After everyone finished posing for pictures with the bear, Cornelius skinned the bear late in the evening, and the town feasted on barbecued meat. Loron Rowley sold the remainder of that "awful, racid"[4] meat in his general store. The saga of the last silver-tipped grizzly found in Southern California south of the Tehachapi Mountains ended with Cornelius making a rug out of the hide and head. His daughters eventually donated it to the Museum of Natural History in Exposition Park, Los Angeles.

Years earlier, sixteen-year-old Cornelius[5] had arrived in the Monte Vista Valley with his father, Farmer, in the early 1800s to cut timber to satisfy Los Angeles's thirst for wood. The cleared land, fertile from dirt washed down the canyon, invited settlement. The Johnsons decided to homestead about 200 acres in Big Tujunga Canyon, part of the San Gabriel Timber Reserve, later to become the Angeles National Forest.[6] Farmer built a small house and sent for his wife and other children, six in all.

As original settlers, the family enjoyed complete

freedom in the canyon. On their ranch, the Johnsons planted vineyards and orchards and kept bees to harvest the honey. In order to irrigate the fruit trees, they dug mile-long ditches along the side of the mountain to divert water from the river. For the hot, dry summers, they built a reservoir.

On the flatter land below, a few other families had also settled in. The Ardizzones and McVines grew grapes; the Bernhardts, grapes and fruit trees; the Adams, olives and peaches; the Wrights, olives; and the Rowleys, fruit. Soon, the Rowleys[7] would open the first general store, and Cornelius's brother John would transform an old hunting lodge into the Monte Vista Inn.[8]

The Johnson's second home on the mesa circa 1912.
Photo courtesy of Glen M. Johnson.

But Farmer's wanderlust prevented him from settling anywhere for too long. After a few years of farming, he decided once again to move on. He sold his land to his sons, Cornelius and John. In his late thirties, Cornelius still lived in the small house built by his father. He seemed content living a simply country life until he met Alice Lee Roybar[9] at the general store.

After losing both her parents to tuberculosis, Alice hoped to find a cure for her own TB. The sixteen-year-old left Iowa and came to live with her great-aunt in the dry, sunny air of Sunland. Her aunt, postmistress Mrs. George Huse, doubled as a correspondent for a Glendale newspaper. She gathered news for her column by reading

The Johnson home many years later as it changed to meet the family's needs.
Photo courtesy of Bolton Hall Museum.

the postcards that came and went in the mail. Alice began studying nursing in Los Angeles, but the physical demands of the job proved too much for her health. Instead, she married the 40-year-old Cornelius in 1908 and went to live in the little house on the slanted mesa. The next year their first daughter, Lucille, arrived.

Three years later Cornelius obtained water rights for the springs up in the mountains. He constructed a pipe system from the springs to irrigate the orchards and to carry water to a new house. With the help of a carpenter, Cornelius built a big, square house further up on the mesa.

Alice's new home included a front room, a dining room, a kitchen with running water, and two bedrooms. The roof extended over a back porch large enough to accommodate a table and chairs. Another little room housed the bath, although toilet facilities remained outside. Instead of the usual galvanized tub with a washboard or wringer, Alice's washing machine operated with a motor turned by water pressure. Electric power in the canyon was years in the future.

Little Lucille helped her father cut wood for the fireplace which kept them warm in winter. In summer, they used a coal oil stove, and coal oil lamps dispensed light. Once a week, her parents shopped in town for groceries; otherwise, they depended on the 'home' orchard of figs, apples, peaches, pomegranates, and oranges for fresh fruit. Cornelius took the grapes from the family's vineyards to Los Angeles markets by horse and buggy, a two-day trip. By 1914, a Buick truck allowed him to drive down to L.A. in the morning and come back the same day. Improved transportation also enabled the family to take a bus and shop in L.A. for clothes.

Like other farm children, Lucille kept busy with chores, especially tending to the chickens. Since no other families lived in the canyon, Lucille had no playmates. She turned to nature for her entertainment and pleasure, thus learning about the flowers and trees and birds. The canyon abounded with wildlife: deer, coyotes, raccoons, skunks,

School picnic in the canyon, June 1910. Photo courtesy of Marshall Murray.

bobcats, ground squirrels, rabbit, snakes, and an occasional mountain lion. But the rattlesnake claimed most of Lucille's attention since it was the most dangerous; other animals tended to be afraid of man and ran away.

Too many encounters, and too many narrow escapes, forced Lucille to learn to deal with the rattlesnakes. She noticed that a rattlesnake can strike only about half its body length, so when the snake stretched out, it was easier

Summertime 1909. Photo courtesy of Marshall Murray.

to kill. A good hard whack with a pitchfork, hoe, gun barrel, shovel, or just a good strong stick, anything sturdy and handy, broke the snake's back and disabled it. The coiled snake was far more dangerous.

Lucille's lonely days ended with the birth of her sister and playmate, Marion, in 1914. They shared many a happy hour with their large collection of dolls. The girls 'sewed' clothes for them by slipping sticks through young, tender alder leaves. Sometimes, they hiked to the river to catch minnows and polliwogs, or they explored the ranch side by side on their horses.

Like all kids, the girls had a mischievous side. When their mother became ill, Cornelius bought some goats, believing the milk would help Alice. When the girls took the goats to the river, they sometimes wandered off, and the girls hid in the brush. Unable to see the girls, the goats panicked and ran for home. Knowing they'd get into trouble because running with bags of milk wasn't good for the goats, the girls hurried to catch up with the goats before they reached home.

When Lucille started school in Sunland's one-room schoolhouse, she walked five miles round-trip each day. By the time she reached fourth grade and Marion was in primary, the school had expanded to two rooms: one teacher for grades one through four, and another teacher for grades five through eight. In the schoolyard, all the children, male and female, played together. The younger children liked to play Indians; the older ones favored baseball, hopscotch, and jacks. At lunch they sometimes hiked down to the wash. The children loved the lavish holiday celebrations at school, especially Halloween, and performing in plays and musicals.

Alice died when Lucille was 12 and Marion 7. The death of a mother is a blow to any child, but in context of the family's isolation in the canyon and the demands of running a ranch, the family missed her all the more. Lucille stepped in to help her father.

Lucille attended Glendale High School for two years. After the City of L.A. annexed Sunland in 1926, Lucille had to transfer to the city high school in San Fernando where she studied economics, cooking, and sewing. High school meant long days; Lucille left home at 6:30 a.m. to catch a bus and didn't get back until 4:00 or 5:00 p.m. Marion missed her sister, her friend and companion, on those long days. While Lucille had spent the early years of her childhood without a playmate, Marion had always had her big sister.

Because of the distance and travel time, few Sunland students participated in extra-curricular activities at the high school. They relied on local activities to socialize. Teens did not date as couples; they planned group activities, often through the church, or went to parties or on hikes. Sometimes they went boating at Lancasters Lake, to dances, or to the movie house in Tujunga.

To avoid the long commute to San Fernando High during her last year, Lucille attended Glendale High. She lived in Glendale by working for room and board and a small salary and only came home on weekends.

After graduation, the girls from the canyon followed

The 1982 flood washed out the road across the canyon, stranding the residents of Riverwood Ranch. Photo courtesy of Bolton Hall Museum.

different paths. Lucille stayed home, caring for the house and doing chores around the ranch, as she'd done for years. One day she called a plumber to repair a problem and met her future husband, Albert Fletcher, whom she married in 1929. Marion returned to the ranch until she met her husband at the Sunland Baptist Church. They married in 1933. Unlike Lucille, Marion worked at jobs outside the home most of her life.

During World War II, Lockheed constantly needed workers to keep pace with their growth spurt. With so many men at war, the plant hired women to fill the jobs. When Marion had worked at the Adams Olive Cannery, men did certain jobs, women did others. For the first time, Marion worked side by side with men at the same job. Because of the women, the company put restrictions on the men's behavior, such as forbidding swearing.

With the sexes thrown together, both doing the same work, Marion witnessed the birth of the "equal work—equal pay" struggle as women grasped the unfairness of their lower pay scale. Later, at Rocketdyne, she discovered a different version of the same problem. The company paid employees according to their classification—and always gave women a different classification than the men. For the same amount of work, for the same skilled labor, the lower classification meant lower wages.

Marion credited the growth of local trailer parks to the

growth of Lockheed during the war years. So many jobs opened that the company also hired from out of state. Local housing could not handle the influx of new people, and trailer parks opened as alternative housing.

Lucille and Marion loved the canyon of their youth: a place of natural beauty crowded with trees and flowers, a running river feeding groves and orchards, wild animals scampering through the brush. The earthquake of February 9, 1971, completely destroyed their childhood home, where Lucille and Albert still lived. The house had been built over a full basement. During the earthquake, the cement foundation crumbled and the whole house slid into the basement, shattering dishes and overturning furniture. When the shaking stopped, the roof was only a foot and a half above the ground. The chimney also collapsed, but not one window broke when the house fell to its doom. Fortunately, no one was hurt, and they later removed their possessions through a window.

Perhaps the destruction of the house paralleled the fate of the canyon. For over a century, man cut down trees, caused fires, and hunted away the wildlife without concern. In the 1900s, Mother Earth answered man's exploitation of the watershed with water shortages in summer and floods in winter. Boulders and sand washed down mountainsides once dense with trees and filled with nature's bounty.

Big Tujunga Canyon with snowcapped mountains.
Both Big Tujunga Canyon and Little Tujunga Canyon were popular
destinations for pleasure trips and for hunting parties,
whether for sport or for food.
Photo courtesy of Bolton Hall Museum.

It really does snow occasionally in Southern California.
Looking north on Eldora after the storm in January 1949.
Photo courtesy of Marshall Murray.

Half a Century Later

The Great Depression dislodged many families who searched for a new beginning. Nobe and Zelda Webber joined the migratory flow when they packed up their belongings and their two-year-old son Larry and left Utah in 1939. They headed south for Los Angeles, in hopes a larger city would offer them better opportunity. Initially, they landed in Glendale where the city rented spaces with stoves in the park. While there, they learned via the grapevine that Dr. Oatey, a Glendale osteopath, needed someone to take care of his ranch in Big Tujunga Canyon.

After some initial discussion, the doctor drove up to their space in the park one day and asked how long it would take them to pack. Zelda replied, "Ten minutes," and quickly gathered up the family's meager belongings. They piled into the doctor's car and headed for Sunland and the canyon.

Up Oro Vista, two miles north of town, they crossed Big Tujunga River. There, nestled in a little valley between two hills, they found their new home. A creek meandered among the ranch buildings: a cabin for them, one the doctor used as a weekend retreat, plus a couple of storage sheds.

Fortunately, Zelda was no stranger to hard work. At age 15, after her father died of cancer, she quit school and went to work in a milk-canning factory to support her mother and six-year-old twin sisters. She'd need her stamina living in a canyon that offered as few amenities in 1939 as it did to the Johnsons half a century earlier. In return for their room and board, the Webbers' duties included taking care of their house and the doctor's, preparing meals for him and his guests, and taking care of the ranch.

Electricity was still a stranger in the canyon; pumps or tanks of gas generated energy. Anyone living in the canyon knew to be prepared. The primitive roads still meandered back and forth across the river. When it rained, the river rose, blocking access to the other side and stranding everyone for days on end. Without telephones to call for help, neighbors relied on each other.

On Saturdays, Dr. Oatey generally brought groceries from the list Zelda had made the week before, although much of what they ate came from the ranch itself. Zelda often served chicken or rabbit for dinner, sometimes turkey or squabs, all garnished with dressing. From the berry patches, she made jam and pies. Favorites were pumpkin, apple, or boysenberry. She also made cakes, especially banana, fudge, ice cream, and root beer soda. When the doctor came to the ranch alone, he usually ate with the Webbers. If he brought guests, Zelda served them in the doctor's cabin.

Larry Webber. If you lived in the canyon, you learned to ride a horse.
Photo courtesy of Zelda Webber.

Any additional

needs, whether groceries or mail or a newspaper, meant saddling the horse for a trip to the general store on Oro Vista and Fenwick, or to the Shopping Bag on Foothill Boulevard. When Larry started kindergarten at Sunland School, Zelda usually took him on horseback too.

A trip to town might actually have offered a welcome relief from the constant rounds of housework: sweeping, dusting, picking-up, cooking, and the inevitable dishes. Piles of clothes always wanted to be washed or ironed or patched. Once Zelda's cabin sparkled, then it was time to turn her attention to the doctor's. And, of course, the once-in-a-while jobs waited: beating rugs, mopping and scrubbing and waxing floors, washing curtains and windows, or varnishing furniture.

If the cabins didn't call for attention, then the outside did. Late fall and winter months focused on cleaning, construction, and repairs. While Nobe handled most of the heavier work, Zelda and Larry pitched in to help. Nobe might dig post holes, set the posts, stretch the wire for fencing around the animal corrals, gardens or along the road, but when he finally put the gate in place, Zelda and Larry picked up the paint cans to finish it.

Brush needed to be cleared, hauled to a safe spot, and burned. Rains always showered the ground with more than moisture. Wood that washed down the mountain had to be cleared out of the way. Rain also washed dirt and sand into

248

the spring. Nobe tried covering it with a screen and putting protective rocks around it, but nothing completely alleviated the necessity of cleaning it. Nobe patched roofs and fixed leaks in the water pipes.

The Angeles National Golf Club, built at the mouth of the wash in 2004, lost two greens to floods a year later.

April showers may bring May flowers, but only with lots of assistance. Nobe rolled up his sleeves to plow and fertilize the fields for sunflowers, kale, corn, and alfalfa. He broke up the hardened ground around the fruit trees and boysenberry patches to aerate the soil. Zelda planted sweet peas, poppies, and tomatoes in the garden he prepared for her. The whole family hiked up the hill to cut hay, which they brought back to the barn for storage.

New or repaired fences protected the plants from ranch animals, but not the wilder creatures looking for food. They shot birds stealing berries or poisoned or trapped squirrels. Rabbit hunting supplied meat for dinner. The rattlesnakes they killed to protect themselves.

The surplus of water in winter became a shortage during summer. The orchards, gardens, and berry patches needed to be watered and weeded. Harvesting and preserving filled the days in late summer and fall. Tending to the animals—goats, calves, rabbits, chickens, turkeys, and horses—was a year-round activity. Besides the essentials like feeding them or milking the goats, Nobe built pens and sheds with cement floors. These required cleaning and spraying several times a year. Fences kept most of the animals safely in corrals, except for the horses, who managed to wander off from time to time. When that happened, the family stopped all other activity to go searching for them. For the winter, Zelda made blankets for the horses; in the summer, Nobe created a shaded area outside the hot barn.

Of course, life was not all work. The Webbers enjoyed horseback riding on secluded trails, surrounded by the natural beauty of the canyon wilderness. Friends came to visit and stayed for dinner or a card game, usually pinochle, or they reciprocated the visits. They danced to the wind-up phonograph or played games like Chinese checkers. Sometimes they went to town to listen to fights, football games, or the World Series on the radio, or to watch a live baseball game in Sunland Park. Larry preferred playing on the swings. From Sunland, they caught a bus to the movies in either Tujunga or Glendale, to watch the popular Shirley Temple or other stars on

Larry and his dog with debris from the storm.
Photo courtesy of Zelda Webber.

the big screen.

On their days off, about one per month, time permitted car trips to Hollywood, Santa Monica, and other points of interest in Los Angeles. January brought the Rose Parade and its fabulous floats, which remain on display after the parade for those who want a closer look. For these simple pleasures, and the security of home and good nourishment, they exchanged all their hard work on the ranch. For the year 1939, they received a total of $85 in cash for services rendered. It was not the labor, but the tragedies to come, that would change their desire to continue living in the canyon.

On January 7, 1940, a roar from the canyon awoke Nobe. He rose to investigate, but could see nothing through the dark curtain of night and the driving rain. The continuing clamor was enough to tell him all was not well, so he awoke Zelda. Grabbing Larry, they ran out of the house and up the hill in their nightclothes. They reached safety just as a wall of water crashed down the canyon.

Huddled together for warmth against the cold night air, they waited until daylight to return to the house. The swollen river had followed the creek down the mountain and washed away everything in its path. Gone was the shed closest to the creek that was used to store the doctor's furniture. Gone was the wood pile for the fireplace. Gone were the animal pens and corrals, although the cows, horses, and goats had managed to escape and survive. In only a few hours, nature asserted its dominance over man's attempts to contain it. Boulders, mud, and debris replaced a year's worth of labor building, repairing, and cleaning.

The storm totally stranded the Webbers. Rocks and boulders so completely blocked the roads that it would take the county weeks to build a new one. Large, rolling waves swept down the river, negating any thought of crossing it. Water; water everywhere—except where they needed it. The storm cut off their water supply, so they were forced to collect rain water for drinking until the river became passable and they could buy it in town. Finally, they managed to reach neighbors and notify Dr. Oatey who left a patient on the table, grabbed his hat, and headed for the ranch. Before they could even consider rebuilding, they faced the mud—everywhere, covering everything.

Only two months later, around noon on March 25, 1940, Larry fell while playing with his dog and slashed his hand between the thumb and finger. While Zelda wrapped his hand in a towel, Nobe hooked the horse to the cart, and they drove to Sunland where they waited for the Glendale bus to get to a doctor. The driver of a passing car saw their obvious distress, stopped, and offered them a ride.

When Dr. Oatey saw Larry's hand, he immediately

took him to a specialist. So horrific was the wound, that the surgeon required the parents to sign a form releasing him from liability if Larry lost use of his thumb. The parents waited fearfully through the long afternoon hours. After darkness fell, Larry woke up. He hand remained bandaged for a long time, while his parents awaited the outcome. When Dr. Oatey finally took the stitches out during a trip to the ranch, everyone breathed a sigh of relief. His thumb not only worked, but it worked well enough not to interfere with his future success as a dentist.

The Tujunga Wash during the dry season.

After the scare from lack of emergency medical services and the traumatic experience with the flood, Zelda refused to live through another year in the canyon. The Webbers stayed over the summer until the rains started, but on October 2, 1940, they moved to Glendale, where Zelda and Nobe gave Larry a brother, Terry, and a sister, Sally. Nobe died five years after their move at age 39 from appendicitis. Left with three children, two of them babies, Zelda searched for employment. She decided on housework, because she could set her own hours and be

The wash during the 1938 flood.
Photo courtesy of Bolton Hall Museum.

home when the kids returned from school. Like his brother Larry, Terry became a dentist and opened a practice in Montrose.

#####

Footnotes

[1] See *Hotels of the Hopeful*, Volume 1 of *The Early History of Sunland, California*.

[2] Sources vary as to whether this was late October or early November.

[3] *The Record-Ledger*, Historical & Progress Edition, May 21, 1953.

[4] "Was Tujunga Bear Country?" *The Leader*, October 31, 1984.

[5] Cornelius Johnson: born October 18, 1867 – died November 4, 1941.

[6] When the San Gabriel Timber Reserve became the Angeles National Forest in 1892, homesteading was no longer allowed.

[7] See *From Crackers to Coal Oil*, Volume 4 of *The Early History of Sunland, California*.

[8] See *Hotels of the Hopeful*, Volume 1 of *The Early History of Sunland, California*.

[9] Alice Lee Roybar: years approximated at 1892 to 1921.

Bibliography

"$1000 Shot." *The Record-Ledger*, Historical & Progress Edition, May 21, 1953.

"Boulevard Only Route to Los Angeles for Early Settlers." *The Record-Ledger*, October 5, 1961.

Cornelius B. Johnson. Funeral record. Bade Mortuary, Tujunga, CA. November 4, 1941.

"Earthquake Ruins Home of Early Local Settler." *The Record-Ledger*, September 27, 1971.

Hitt, Marlene. "Early Settlers Witnessed Some Cataclysmic Changes." *The Foothill Leader*, May 29-30, 1999.

Hitt, Marlene. "Tujunga Settler Shot the Last Grizzly Bear." *The Foothill Leader*, August 21-22, 1999.

Lombard, Sarah. "Mining and Water Claims Embedded in History." *The Record-Ledger*, September 29, 1977.

Lombard, Sarah. "Tujunga Wash—Wilderness Close at Hand." *The Record-Ledger*, October 6, 1977.

"Lucille and Marion Johnson: Two Women from the Canyon." Oral history recorded by Julia Stein. Bolton Hall Museum.

"Old Days on the Big Tujunga." *Trails Magazine*: Vol. 5, No. 1. Winter, 1938.

"Paul Johnson, Born in Big Tujunga Canyon in 1900, Dies at 53." *The Record-Ledger*, December 10, 1953.

Robinson, John W. *The San Gabriels.* Arcadia, CA: Big Santa Anita Historical Society, 1991.

"Saga of Monte Vista." *The Record-Ledger*, Thursday, June 18, 1864.

Tiernan, Mary Lee. *From Crackers to Coal Oil.* Sunland, CA: Snoops Desktop Publishing, 1999.

Tiernan, Mary Lee. *Hotels for the Hopeful.* Sunland, CA: Snoops Desktop Publishing, 1999.

"Was Tujunga Bear Country?" *The Leader*, October 31, 1984.

Webber, Zelda. Personal diary: 1939-1943.

Webber, Zelda. Person interview by Mary Lee Tiernan. July 16, 1999.

From Whence They Came

"The boom of the '80s burst...
But settlers continued to drift into the valley
and to plant vineyards and orchards...
the little community of Sunland developed."

*The Early History of Sunland, California
Volume 8*

ML Tiernan

The Land Boom of the 1880s brought immigrants from around the world. Two generations of Blumfields survived the difficulties of farming and water shortages through industry and imagination.

From Whence They Came

From foreign country or neighboring town
they settled in the valley and changed
a ghost town[1] into a community.

The Early History of Sunland, California
Volume 8

ML Tiernan

From Whence They Came

www.maryleetiernan.com
Second printing April 1, 2015
10 9 8 7 6 5 4 3 2

ISBN 978-0983067276 (Paperback)

Photograph on cover courtesy of A. Elizabeth Schell. Quote on cover from "Sunland First Developed in Big 1887 Land Boom."

Contents

Coming to Sunland

After the great Land Boom of the 1880s[2] ended, settlers continued to migrate to California, not for gold, but for oranges and warm weather. The famous Pasadena Tournament of Roses began in 1890 as part of the new strategy to promote Southern California. And what could

William and Amelia Adams Blumfield.
Photos courtesy of A. Elizabeth Schell.

advertise the temperate climate better than staging an outdoor parade with fresh flowers in the middle of winter? Many of these new civic-minded pioneers had the means to improve the lands they bought. Settlers of moderate means tended to migrate to the country areas outside Los Angeles.

Amelia Blumfield[3] wasn't thinking about oranges or warm weather or even gold; she just plain missed her family. Years earlier, in 1873, Amelia, her husband William[4], and their four children had left England and migrated to Canada to join some of her twelve brothers and sisters. They'd managed all right in Canada: William working as a carpenter, she as a midwife. She'd earned about $2.40 a week caring for newborns and their mothers.

But by 1894, her brothers[5] and sister, and even one daughter, had moved on to California, and she missed them. When news of the birth of her grandson[6] in Pasadena arrived, that, and the lure of the low $12 railroad rates to California, seemed good enough reasons to pack up her family and their possessions once more. Out came the pine trunk William had made for their trip to Canada.[7]

Like many who came to California to visit, Amelia and William decided to stay. They bought twenty acres of land, dotted with clusters of oak trees, in the small community of Sunland, where her youngest brother Alfred Adams lived. The village, which only had one store[8], had been renamed Sunland in 1887 because the postal officials refused to accept the name Monte Vista. The town of "Monta" Vista already existed, and they decided the similar spellings of "Monta" and "Monte" would cause confusion. Why the name Sunland? M.V. Hartranft, a land developer in the early 1900s wrote in a sales brochure: "They (Verdugo Mountains) roll back the fog banks from the sea, much as you would raise a curtain to let the sunshine in—and the early settlers called it Sunland. Which it is."[9]

The Blumfield land, adjacent to the center of town, stretched from Hillrose Street north to Wentworth Street

Amelia and William's first home under the oaks. Picture dates prior to 1905. Photo courtesy of A. Elizabeth Schell.

and from Sherman Grove Avenue east approximately 600feet. With plenty of wood available, William set to work using his carpentry skills and built a house on Hillrose in the shade of the oak trees.[10]

Amelia watched eagerly as William erected their two-story home. She envisioned the many hours they would relax in their easy chairs looking out the bay window in the living room. When company came, the spacious room accommodated a large dining table, although they tended to eat most meals in the kitchen. In addition to a bedroom, a special room also shared the ground floor space, for William planned built-in luxuries for Amelia's new house. Her kitchen featured a sink with running water, and the special room housed a wood-framed bathtub lined with metal.

Under the stairs to the two upstairs rooms, William built a pantry. Years later Amelia's grandchildren would remember her taking homemade bread from that pantry and, holding it against herself, cut off a slice. After spreading it with home-churned butter, she sprinkled sugar on top as a treat.

Amelia lovingly cared for her new home. To clean the bare pine wood floors, she took damp tea leaves from the ever-present tea pot and sprinkled them on the floor to keep the dust down while she swept.

Besides building their home and doing other paid carpentry jobs, William worked in the local olive groves until he could clear his own land. Slowly, with help from relatives and neighbors[11], the Blumfields prepared the land and planted it with apricot and peach trees, and later grape vines. A 500 gallon tank in the backyard stored water from Big Tujunga Canyon which they pumped into the orchard.

Early Sunland farmers depended on water from Big Tujunga Canyon to irrigate the dry land. They formed a cooperative, the Mutual Water Company, and built irrigation ditches to carry the water to their groves. The company charged either time or money for the amount of

Elizabeth and Russ on their little red chairs.
Photo courtesy of A. Elizabeth Schell.

water each member used on a monthly basis. Money bought needed materials. Time meant working on the line and making repairs, a never-ending project given the poor condition of the pipes and the constant breakage. The flume through the Blumfield orchards ran east from Sherman Grove, then curved around heading south to Hillrose Street. Its path approximates Forsythe Street.

Behind the house stood a barn with horse stalls and a shed for hay where Amelia raised turkeys. They proved to be challenging and difficult to raise. Their son Alfred worked alongside William for twelve years, clearing and planting the land and tending the orchard until his marriage in 1906. When he married, Amelia and William gave Alfred and his wife one acre of land on Sherman Grove as a wedding present. Amelia's grandchildren arrived shortly thereafter.

The grandchildren, Russ and Elizabeth, loved to visit their grandparents. They would drag their little red chairs almost daily over the sandy path between their house and their grandparents'. Amelia always welcomed them with the door opened wide. Should they arrive at mealtime, they seated themselves on their red chairs while Grandfather said a blessing. Believing children should not drink the strong tea that the adults did, Grandmother served them a special 'tea,' a mixture of hot water and milk, which they hated. The children dragged the chairs back and forth so often that the sandy path ground the ends of the legs down to points.

The site of Amelia's first home in Sunland, however, was not well-chosen. During the winter, the shade from the oaks proved too much for the iron wood-heating stove. If the cold winters weren't enough, the threat of the mighty oaks was. Twenty-nine years earlier, when William had built the house, he laid the foundation among the trees. In 1894, enough room lay between the house and the trees to permit passage in-between, but by 1923, after years of growth, the oaks threatened to brush aside man's feebler structure and claim the ground for itself. Amelia's beloved home was torn down and the lumber used to build a new home in a sunnier location. It was still on Hillrose, but closer to Sherman Grove Avenue.

During the early years of Hollywood, producers often chose the rustic scenery of Sunland, especially Sunland Park and Lancasters Lake, for set locations. The children— all the local kids as well as Russ and Elizabeth—loved climbing around the sets and watching the shoots. Many remember a kind actor or actress who took the time to entertain them. One cowboy, after galloping up and down the hills, stopped and swung Elizabeth up on the saddle for a ride on his horse. Or those movie-making days might even have given them their own special moment on the silver screen. In Mary Pickford's film *Heart of the Hills*, a local boy named Jack James was chosen to fight with Mary in a scene where, as the new girl in school, the kids were making fun of her and she fights back. The 'school' was actually the old church in the park. Many of the children appeared as extras in various films; Elizabeth once received 50¢ to appear in a crowd.

Adults also shared a moment of 'fame and glory' as extras, for which they received as much as $5.00 a day and a box lunch. One script called for a scene of early days and Grandmother Amelia fit the bill perfectly with her hair piled in a bun and her high-necked dresses, which always hung a little longer than the current style. After her debut on the silver screen, she good-naturedly accepted teasing for participating—she who had denounced moving pictures and playing cards as sinful.

Amelia and William celebrated 60 years of marriage before William's death in 1927. Through all those years together, they retained a faint trace of the accent they brought with them from England. Amelia died shortly before her 95th birthday in 1940. She deeded five acres of her property to her daughter Amelia Blumfield (Millie) Tench, and the remaining 14 acres to her son Alfred. The property has since been subdivided for houses. But before that happened, the next generation had its story to tell.

The Next Generation

At the Roscoe depot, a young woman climbed down from the train which paused just long enough to unload the mail and one passenger—herself. The fresh, clean air revived her after the long ride in the stuffy train car. Then she remembered her purpose in coming and her hands shook slightly. A properly dressed gentleman approached, introduced himself as Mr. Rowley, one of the school trustees, and escorted her to a horse and buggy.

They bumped up the hillside on a dirt road, jack rabbits scurrying out of their way. When they finally reached the crest of Watson's Hill[12], she gasped at the beauty of the valley lying before her. But as the distance closed between them and the little village of Sunland, her stomach began to tighten.

After graduating from ninth grade and then the Normal School in Los Angeles, a training institute for teachers, Clara Freeman[13] had come all the way from Downey to apply for a teaching position. The distance may not have been quite as far as her parents had traveled. Her

Clara and Alfred Blumfield on their wedding day in 1906.
Photo courtesy of A. Elizabeth Schell.

father's family originally came from Cape Cod, Massachusetts to Nebraska, and then years later her parents migrated to California. But in those days, for a young woman striking out on her own, it was quite an adventure.

Mr. Rowley drove past the one-room schoolhouse in the northeast corner of Sunland Park—which was about half its current size. It would be many years yet before William Bernhard, another original settler, would donate a parcel of his land to enlarge the park. Clara's knees trembled at the sight of the school and the thought of the impending interview with the other members of the board.

Finally the moment arrived when they stopped in front of the home of Alfred Adams Jr. whose eight children would keep the schoolroom filled for many years. Clara recounted her training and experience, answered their questions, and soon found herself back in the buggy for the four-and-a-half mile ride back to the train. Several days later an offer arrived, and Clara once more boarded the train for Sunland.

During that first year of teaching in 1904, Clara boarded with the Alfred Adams Sr. family and walked three blocks to the one-room school in Sunland Park.[14] Although the exact number of students in Clara's class is unknown, attendance during this period varied from an average of 12 to a high of 20. Transients, attracted by the valley's climate, came and camped for six months to a year at a time. The attendance, or not, of their children caused the fluctuation in enrollment. Sometimes two or three students would be in the same grade level; other times, none. Clara taught all eight grade levels.[15]

Also during her first year, Alfred Tunstill Blumfield[16], another one of the trustees, began courting Clara by never missing the opportunity to drive her back and forth to the Roscoe depot for trips home to visit her family in Downey. During Clara's second year of teaching, she lived with

Clara and Alfred's home at 10738 Sherman Grove Avenue.
Photo courtesy of their daughter A. Elizabeth Schell.

Captain and Mrs. Cushman. Her romance with Alfred blossomed and they decided to marry; Clara was 23, Alfred 27. For their wedding in June 1906, the Cushmans returned Clara's final month's room and board as a wedding present. With this money, the couple bought a piano, which their descendants still use. Alfred's parents, William and Amelia, deeded one of their 20 acres to them. After their honeymoon in Catalina, the couple returned to their new home, built on that acre by Alfred's father and Clara's father, Charles Russell Freeman. Clara and Alfred would spend the next fifty years there, at 10738 Sherman Grove Avenue. The house still stands, as of this writing in

In 2001, the Blumfield house still stood as one of the few structures left from Sunland's earliest days, but not in the best condition.

2001, although in rather deplorable condition.

After her marriage, Clara gave up her teaching position. Alfred and Clara's two children arrived in quick succession: William Russell (Russ) in 1907 and Elizabeth in 1908.[17] Fortunately, instead of a midwife, Clara found a doctor living in the Monte Vista Hotel who delivered both her children in her home on Sherman Grove. Unfortunately, the doctor was from out-of-state and had no California license. Consequently, he failed to report and register the births of her children, leaving them both without birth certificates. In later years, they had some difficulty officially proving that they existed.

For the next twenty-five years or so, Alfred cared for the Wright's olive groves as his primary employment. Although Mr. Wright owned the land stretching north to Hillrose and south to Foothill Boulevard, between McVine on the east and Woodward on the west, he did not live in the valley and left the care of his groves and the harvesting of the olives in the fall in Alfred's capable hands.

Alfred's work necessitated frequent trips to Los Angeles, where he often did the family shopping. Because only about fifty families lived in all of Sunland and Tujunga, few stores existed in the village. When Clara wanted to do her own shopping, she brought the children all the way to Downey on the train to their other set of grandparents and then back again. The long trip with young children meant that it didn't happen too often.

A strong work ethic challenged American settlers, or they would not have accomplished what they did. They continually sought new opportunities to assure a better living for their families and passed that ethic on to their children. As Russ remembers, "My dad always said, 'You can do jobs for me,' so I had to cultivate and hoe. I made

Irene Lancaster, a neighbor, with the Blumfield home in the background. Irene died at age 21 in the 1918-1919 flu pandemic that claimed over 20 million lives. Photo courtesy of Marshall Murray.

my money for my clothes and stuff for school the next year. It helped out—which you had to do in those days."[18]

So in addition to Alfred's steady job working the Wright olive groves, the young couple also helped with William's orchard. After bringing home part of the day's harvest, Alfred and Clara sorted the fruit at night under the huge live oak in the backyard and packed the best fruit for market. The next day, the fruit would be hauled to Los Angeles wholesale sheds. The arrival of electricity around 1913 helped ease the annual sorting task. A long cord from the house to the yard provided light for the night ritual.

During World War I, Alfred rented vineyards from the McVine family, and Clara and the kids spent long days in the vineyards helping to pick grapes. Income from the harvest financed the family's first car, a Model T Ford. Clara also worked in the Adams Olive Cannery and later at the Monte Vista Hotel, after its conversion to a home for the elderly. She served on the election board and as clerk of the school board, issuing teachers' paychecks. After updating her credential at the University of Southern California, she returned to teaching for two years, in 1919 and 1920, to the same one-room classroom she had left years before. Only this time the old classroom was used as the second classroom in the new two-room Sunland School on Hillrose Street where Clara taught the lower grades.

During heavy rains, water cascaded down Haines

Canyon, formed a river as it crossed Hillrose, and flooded the park. When that happened, both teacher and students enjoyed a surprise holiday because the flood denied anyone access to the school. Sometimes, however, an unexpected storm brought heavy rains while school was in session, trapping the children in the schoolhouse. Crossing the turbulent waters was dangerous, especially for the younger children. Elizabeth remembers such a storm when she was six; the big boys in the upper grades solved the problem by carrying the smaller children across the flooded field to safety. At other times, the children waited for their parents to arrive on horseback to rescue them. The

Looking north on Sherman Grove Avenue circa 1937, one of the few paved streets in Sunland. The Blumfield house is on the right, past the trees. Photo courtesy of Marshall Murray.

flooding in the park is why Sunland School was eventually moved to the site on Hillrose Street above the water crossing.

With the money she earned teaching, Clara helped finance the construction of three rental cottages on their acre of land. As farmers, they depended on water for a successful crop, especially during the long, hot summer. However, the water supply was not adequate. Without enough rain to fill the watershed during the year, the river simply dried up. Numerous breakdowns with the piping system from Big Tujunga Canyon also interfered with the water flow, and new settlers in the area meant less water for everyone. Sometimes there just wasn't enough water to ensure a healthy crop. During droughts, crops failed for lack of any water at all. Clara and Alfred relied on the rent from the cottages and from other property they bought and leased as basic income.

Clara's outside activities did not interfere with her duties at home. Without today's machines and conveniences, Clara spent hours cleaning, cooking, doing laundry and other household chores, quilting in the front room by the window, and making clothes for Elizabeth's dolls: dresses, aprons, panties, coats, and hats. Farm duties piled on top of house chores. Clara raised chickens; she gathered the eggs, cleaned and candled[19] them in the cellar beneath the house, and then sold them. She hand-churned ice cream and tended a vegetable garden; the first of her sweet corn became a traditional part of the town's Fourth of July festivities.

Alfred and Clara inherited fourteen more acres from Amelia after her death in 1940. When Russ married, they gave their son and his wife Marcie one acre of land, just as Alfred's parents had done for them. Russ built their house at 10822 Sherman Grove, on the hill overlooking the orchards, north of their parents' home. When their twins were born, knowing the difficulty of handling two small babies, Clara traveled a well-worn path from her house to her daughter-in-law's to help with all the chores.

Russ stayed close to home, but Elizabeth did not. While she was attending Occidental College in 1928, Elizabeth became very good friends with Dorothy Foree from San Luis Obispo, California, and Ellice Thompson, from Cashmere, Washington. In the summer of that year, the three girls ventured north to Cashmere to work in the apple orchards. But Elizabeth found more than apples in Washington. There she met Clarence Schell, who followed Elizabeth home after the harvest. He worked in a fruit warehouse in San Fernando until he could convince the twenty-year-old Elizabeth to marry him. They married on Valentine's Day in 1929 and returned to Cashmere, Washington, later that month.

Elizabeth Blumfield and Clarence Schell at Lancasters Lake
just prior to their marriage in 1929.
Photo courtesy of A. Elizabeth Schell.

The distance and the difficulty of travel did not deter Clara from helping Elizabeth when her daughter gave birth to her own four children. Clara traveled all the way to Washington State to welcome each new grandchild.

Pioneer families worked long and hard to transform the land. In working side by side, they developed a closeness that modern technology has eroded. Thinking fondly of an era when families spent more time together, Elizabeth recalls her childhood Christmases when they strung popcorn and made colored paper chains to decorate

Alfred Blumfield (left) with Russ and Elizabeth in the foreground, unidentified man (center), and Mrs. and Mrs. Leonard McVine (right), other early settlers in Monte Vista, enjoying a bit of free time hunting and camping in Little Tujunga Canyon. Photo courtesy of A. Elizabeth Schell.

the tree. "We also put lighted candles on the tree, though I definitely frown on the practice today."[20]

They also shared their leisure time with neighbors, whether for picnics in the park on a Sunday afternoon, celebrations of holidays and weddings, or by enjoying outdoor life in the nearby Big and Little Tujunga Canyons. Early Sunland hotels thrived on visitors from Los Angeles who came to the 'country' for hunting and hiking in the canyons. Locals, too, took advantage of the bounty at their back door both for relaxation and to supply meat for their tables.

On June 26, 1956, Clara and Alfred celebrated their golden wedding anniversary. The young woman who had nervously descended from the train so many years ago had stepped into the town's history. Clara died less than a year later, and Alfred died in 1962.

#####

Map of Sunland Families:
Where They Lived

Footnotes

[1] Monte Vista is listed in some history books as a "ghost town" because it failed to develop during the Land Boom of the 1880s. See *Hotels for the Hopeful*, Volume 1 of *The Early History of Sunland, California*.

[2] See *Hotels for the Hopeful*.

[3] Amelia Adams Blumfield: born June 1, 1845 – died March 1940.

[4] William Blumfield: born July 31, 1844, - died July 1927.

[5] Her youngest brother Alfred Adams Sr. lived in Sunland. His son Alfred Jr. established the Adams Olive Cannery.

[6] Her daughter Amelia B. (Millie) Blumfield married Frank Tench. Their son, George Tench, was the first to meet Parson Wornum. See *The Parson and His Cemetery*, Volume 3 of *The Early History of Sunland, California*.

[7] The trunk still remains in the family as a treasured heirloom.

[8] See *From Crackers to Coal Oil*, Volume 4 of *The Early History of Sunland, California*.

[9] Hartranft, M.V., *The Western Empire Land-Banking and Home Securing Plan*, Los Angeles, CA: The Fruit World Publishing Co., January 1911, p. 21.

[10] The first house was probably near Russett Avenue, although the street didn't exist then.

[11] Their closest neighbors were the Rowleys who lived on Hillrose between Floralita and Oro Vista.

[12] The hill by the 210 Freeway and Foothill Boulevard in Sunland.

[13] Clara Marie Freeman Blumfield: born March 9, 1883 – died April 6, 1957.

[14] The school was located approximately where the baseball fields were later built.

[15] A picture of the first schoolhouse in Sunland Park is found in *From Crackers to Coal Oil*, Volume 4 of *The Early History of Sunland, California*.

[16] Alfred Tunstill Blumfield: born October 5, 1878 – died February 25, 1962.

[17] William Russell Blumfield: born April 16, 1906 – died June 3, 1983. A. (Alma) Elizabeth Blumfield Schell: born May 2, 1908 – still living as of this writing in 2001.

[18] Blumfield, William Russell. Personal interview by Viola L. Carlson, February 19, 1983.

[19] Clara examined the eggs for freshness by holding them up to a bright light.

[20] Schell, A. Elizabeth, *Early Memories of My Childhood*, July 24, 1983.

Bibliography

"Amelia Blumfield, Sunland Pioneer Called by Death." *The Record Ledger*, March 21, 1940.

Blumfield, William Russell. Personal interview by Viola L. Carlson, February 19, 1983.

"Blumfields Have Resided in Same Home on Sherman Grove Since 1906 Marriage." *The Record Ledger*, Historical & Progress Edition. May 21, 1953,

"First Sunland School Founded About 1898 in 1-Room Building." *The Record Ledger*, Historical & Progress Edition, May 21, 1953.

"Golden Wedding." *Tri-City Progress,* September 17, 1915.

Hartranft, M.V., *The Western Empire Land-Banking and Home Securing Plan*, Los Angeles, CA: The Fruit World Publishing Co., January 1911.

"Pioneer Sunland Teacher Dies at Glendale Hospital." *The Record Ledger*, April 11, 1957.

Schell, A. Elizabeth Blumfield. *Early Memories of My Childhood.* July 24, 1983.

Schell, A. Elizabeth Blumfield. Letter to the Board of Sunland-Tujunga Little Landers Historical Society. June 7, 1994.

Schell, A. Elizabeth Blumfield. Letters to Mary Lee Tiernan. 1999-2001.

Schell, A. Elizabeth Blumfield. *Memories of the Past.*

Schell, A. Elizabeth Blumfield. *Random Ramblings: The Memoirs of A. Elizabeth Blumfield Schell.* Cashmere, Washington, July 1990.

Schell, A. Elizabeth Blumfield. *Trips to California.* 2000.

"Sunland First Developed in Big 1887 Land Boom." *The Record Ledger*, September 12, 1968.

"To Move House Out of Oak Tree's Way." *The Record Ledger*, May 3, 1923.

"Where's Monte(a) Vista?" *The Glendale NewsPress,* April 4, 1968.